GOVERNMENT PROCEDURES AND OPERATIONS

FEDERAL DATA CENTER CONSOLIDATION

SUCCESSES AND CHALLENGES

GOVERNMENT PROCEDURES AND OPERATIONS

Additional books in this series can be found on Nova's website under the Series tab.

Additional e-books in this series can be found on Nova's website under the e-book tab.

GOVERNMENT PROCEDURES AND OPERATIONS

FEDERAL DATA CENTER CONSOLIDATION

SUCCESSES AND CHALLENGES

PATRICIA L. WINSLOW
EDITOR

New York

LIBRARY OF CONGRESS CATALOGING-IN-PUBLICATION DATA

ISBN: 978-1-63463-896-8

Published by Nova Science Publishers, Inc. † New York

CONTENTS

PREFACE

The objectives of this book are to evaluate the extent to which agencies have achieved cost savings to date and identified future savings through their consolidation efforts; identify agencies' notable consolidation successes and challenges in achieving cost savings; and evaluate the extent to which data center optimization metrics have been established.

Chapter 1 – In 2010, as focal point for information technology management across the government, OMB's Federal Chief Information Officer launched the Federal Data Center Consolidation Initiative to consolidate the growing number of centers. As of May 2014, agencies reported a total of 9,658 data centers—approximately 6,500 more than reported by OMB in 2011.

GAO was asked to review federal agencies' continuing efforts to consolidate their data centers and achieve cost savings. The objectives were to (1) evaluate the extent to which agencies have achieved cost savings to date and identified future savings through their consolidation efforts, (2) identify agencies' notable consolidation successes and challenges in achieving cost savings, and (3) evaluate the extent to which data center optimization metrics have been established. GAO assessed agency-reported cost savings and avoidance documentation, interviewed agency officials, and assessed data center optimization metrics against prior OMB requirements and goals.

Chapter 2 – The Department of Defense (DOD) is the single largest energy consumer in the nation. As the largest owner of federal data centers, with 772, the DOD has more than twice as many centers as any other agency. By consolidating some of its data centers, DOD could have a significant positive impact on energy savings for the federal government. DOD has instituted a number of policy directives, as have all federal agencies, that influence energy use in its data centers.

Data centers are facilities—buildings or parts of buildings—used to store, manage, and disseminate electronic information for a computer network. They house servers, which are computers used to perform network-management functions such as data storage and processing, and communications equipment and devices to connect the servers with the network. Data centers usually draw their power from the electric grid, but they may also contain specialized power conversion and backup equipment to maintain reliable power. Power consumption varies greatly among data centers but is typically many times higher than for other kinds of buildings.

Within the context of the FDCCI, DOD's efforts are intended to address concerns about rising energy demands and costs of data centers, associated increases in carbon emissions, expanding real-estate footprints of data centers, and rising real-estate costs. According to DOD, the Department plans to reduce the number of its data centers by about 30% by 2013, and the number of servers by 25%. DOD intends to use savings generated from consolidation to pay the consolidation costs. DOD also plans to use cloud computing as part of its savings effort.

As with any endeavor being implemented across so many departments and agencies, proper management of the initiative will be crucial to its success and, in turn, to achieving the projected savings. Unlike many programs that are overseen by a single committee, implementation of the FDCCI may require oversight by any committee with legislative jurisdiction over a department or agency. Understanding the management challenges and policy considerations involved with data center consolidation (e.g., balancing up-front costs with ongoing savings, maintaining data security, and maximizing energy savings through facilities design) as well as being aware of the issues specific to implementing the FDCCI are important steps to achieving effective Congressional oversight of the FDCCI. In conducting oversight, Congress may wish to

- conduct hearings to monitor the activities of OMB as it manages the FDCCI or the progress of individual departments and agencies as they implement the FDCCI;
- review FDCCI plans and status reports created internally by the individual department or agency, or externally by the Government Accountability Office (GAO) or the committee of jurisdiction.

Finally, Congress may wish to examine the current "reach" of the FDCCI and consider whether expanding the initiative to include other agencies, as GAO has recommended, is appropriate.

In: Federal Data Center Consolidation
Editor: Patricia L. Winslow ISBN: 978-1-63463-896-8

Chapter 1

DATA CENTER CONSOLIDATION: REPORTING CAN BE IMPROVED TO REFLECT SUBSTANTIAL PLANNED SAVINGS*

United States Government Accountability Office

WHY GAO DID THIS STUDY

In 2010, as focal point for information technology management across the government, OMB's Federal Chief Information Officer launched the Federal Data Center Consolidation Initiative to consolidate the growing number of centers. As of May 2014, agencies reported a total of 9,658 data centers—approximately 6,500 more than reported by OMB in 2011.

GAO was asked to review federal agencies' continuing efforts to consolidate their data centers and achieve cost savings. The objectives were to (1) evaluate the extent to which agencies have achieved cost savings to date and identified future savings through their consolidation efforts, (2) identify agencies' notable consolidation successes and challenges in achieving cost savings, and (3) evaluate the extent to which data center optimization metrics have been established. GAO assessed agency-reported cost savings and avoidance documentation, interviewed agency officials, and assessed data center optimization metrics against prior OMB requirements and goals.

---

* This is an edited, reformatted and augmented version of a United States Government Accountability Office publication, No. GAO-14-713, dated September 2014.

WHAT GAO RECOMMENDS

GAO is recommending that OMB assist agencies in reporting cost savings and develop a metric for server utilization as part of any reevaluation of the metrics. GAO is also recommending, among other things, that agencies fully report their consolidation cost savings. OMB and 12 agencies agreed, 1 did not state whether it agreed or disagreed, 1 had no comments, and 1 partially agreed noting challenges. GAO continues to believe the recommendation remains valid as discussed in the report.

WHAT GAO FOUND

Of the 24 agencies participating in the Federal Data Center Consolidation Initiative, 19 agencies collectively reported achieving an estimated $1.1 billion in cost savings and avoidances between fiscal years 2011 and 2013. Notably, the Departments of Defense, Homeland Security, and Treasury accounted for approximately $850 million (or 74 percent) of the total. In addition, 21 agencies collectively reported planning an additional $2.1 billion in cost savings and avoidances by the end of fiscal year 2015, for a total of approximately $3.3 billion—an amount that is about $300 million higher than the Office of Management and Budget's (OMB) original $3 billion goal. Between fiscal years 2011 and 2017, agencies reported planning a total of about $5.3 billion in cost savings and avoidances.

Agencies' Data Center Consolidation Cost Savings and Avoidances (Dollars in Millions)

	Estimated and actual			Planned				
Fiscal year	2011	2012	2013	2014	2015	2016	2017	Total
Total savings and avoidances	$192	$268	$683	$895	$1,250	$917	$1,144	$5,350
	$1,143 total			**$4,206 total**				

Source: GAO analysis of agency data. | GAO-14-713 Note: Totals may not add due to rounding.

However, planned savings may be higher because six agencies that reported having closed as many as 67 data centers reported limited or no savings, in part because they encountered difficulties, such as calculating baseline data center costs. In addition, 11 of the 21 agencies with planned cost savings are underreporting their fiscal years 2012 through 2015 figures to OMB by approximately $2.2 billion. While several agencies noted communication issues as the reason for this, others did not provide a reason. Until OMB assists agencies in reporting savings and agencies fully report their savings, the $5.3 billion in total savings will be understated.

Most agencies reported successes in achieving cost savings—notably, the benefits of key technologies, reduced power consumption and facility costs, and improvements in asset inventories. However, agencies also reported challenges, many of which were the same as GAO found in 2012. One of the most-reported challenges was related to obtaining power usage information as a means to determine cost savings. In light of how closely these successes and challenges relate to achieving cost savings, it is important for OMB to continue to provide leadership and guidance, including—as GAO previously recommended—using the Data Center Consolidation Task Force to monitor agencies' efforts.

Pursuant to OMB guidance, in May 2014 the Data Center Consolidation Task Force completed a set of 11 metrics to measure agency progress toward optimizing their data centers, such as power usage and facility utilization. In addition, related targets to be achieved by fiscal year 2015 have been developed for nearly all the metrics. However, the metrics do not address server utilization, even though OMB reported this to be as low as 5 percent in 2009, which is significantly below OMB's target of 60 to 70 percent. Without such a metric, OMB may not be getting important insight into agencies' progress on a key issue that was a driving factor in launching the consolidation initiative.

ABBREVIATIONS

CIO	chief information officer
DHS	Department of Homeland Security
EPA	Environmental Protection Agency
FDCCI	Federal Data Center Consolidation Initiative
GPRAMA	Government Performance and Results Act Modernization Act of 2010
GSA	General Services Administration
HHS	Department of Health and Human Services
HUD	Department of Housing and Urban Development

IT	information technology
NASA	National Aeronautics and Space Administration
NRC	Nuclear Regulatory Commission
NSF	National Science Foundation
OMB	Office of Management and Budget
OPM	Office of Personnel Management
SBA	Small Business Administration
SSA	Social Security Administration
Task Force	Data Center Consolidation Task Force
USAID	U.S. Agency for International Development
VA	Department of Veterans Affairs

* * *

September 25, 2014

Congressional Requesters

The federal government's demand for information technology (IT) is ever increasing. In recent years, as federal agencies have modernized their operations, put more of their services online, and increased their information security profiles, their need for computing power and data storage resources has increased. Over time, this increasing demand led to a dramatic rise in the number of federal data centers and a corresponding increase in operational costs. In response, the Office of Management and Budget's (OMB) Federal Chief Information Officer (CIO) launched the Federal Data Center Consolidation Initiative (FDCCI) in 2010.

During the past several years, we reported[1] and testified[2] that, while data center consolidation could potentially save the federal government billions of dollars, weaknesses existed in the execution and oversight of the initiative. Specifically, in July 2011 and July 2012, we reported that nearly all of the 24 departments and agencies (agencies) participating in FDCCI[3] had not yet completed a data center inventory or the consolidation plans to implement their consolidation initiative. More recently, in April 2013, we found that OMB's oversight of the initiative had shortcomings, including that the agency was not tracking and reporting cost savings. As a result, we recommended that OMB require agencies to complete their missing inventory and plan elements and improve the execution of important oversight responsibilities, among other things. Subsequently, OMB and agencies took actions to address these deficiencies, which are discussed later in this report.

Given the importance of the consolidation initiative, you asked that we review federal agencies' continuing efforts to consolidate their data centers and achieve cost savings. Specifically, our objectives were to (1) evaluate the extent to which agencies have achieved cost savings to date and identified future savings through their consolidation efforts, (2) identify agencies' notable consolidation successes and challenges in achieving cost savings, and (3) evaluate the extent to which data center optimization metrics have been established.

To address our first objective, we obtained and analyzed the 24 FDCCI agencies' cost savings and avoidance documentation, such as cost models, budget and contract documentation, and quarterly status reports to OMB. Then, we identified the total agency-reported savings achieved from fiscal years 2011 to 2013 and planned from fiscal years 2014 through 2017. We also compared agency documentation to data center consolidation cost savings and avoidance reporting requirements outlined in a March 2013 OMB memorandum.[4] To address our second objective, we reviewed all 24 agencies' documentation and interviewed agency officials to determine what consolidation successes have been realized in achieving cost savings and what challenges have been faced in achieving cost savings. Finally, for our third objective, we compared the established data center optimization metrics to the requirements for such metrics, as documented in OMB's March 2013 memorandum,[5] and interviewed OMB, General Services Administration (GSA), and Data Center Consolidation Task Force (Task Force) officials to discuss the process by which the metrics were established and to determine the extent to which related targets for the metrics had been established. We also compared the established metrics against areas identified by OMB in prior data center consolidation-related memorandums and guidance as having importance to data center optimization.

We conducted this performance audit from October 2013 to September 2014 in accordance with generally accepted government auditing standards. Those standards require that we plan and perform the audit to obtain sufficient, appropriate evidence to provide a reasonable basis for our findings and conclusions based on our audit objectives. We believe that the evidence obtained provides a reasonable basis for our findings and conclusions based on our audit objectives. Appendix I contains further details about our objectives, scope, and methodology.

BACKGROUND

The federal government's increasing demand for IT led to a dramatic rise in the number of federal data centers and a corresponding increase in operational costs. According to OMB, the federal government had 432 data centers in 1998 and more than 1,100 in 2009. Operating such a large number of centers has been and continues to be a significant cost to the federal government, including costs for hardware, software, real estate, and cooling. For example, in 2007, the Environmental Protection Agency (EPA) estimated that the electricity cost to operate federal servers and data centers across the government was about $450 million annually. According to the Department of Energy (Energy), data center spaces can consume 100 to 200 times more electricity than a standard office space. In 2009, OMB reported[6] that server utilization rates as low as 5 percent across the federal government's estimated 150,000 servers were a driving factor in the need to establish a coordinated, government-wide effort to improve the efficiency, performance, and environmental footprint of federal data center activities.

OMB and the Federal CIO Established the Federal Data Center Consolidation Initiative

Concerned about the size of the federal data center inventory and the potential to improve the efficiency, performance, and the environmental footprint of federal data center activities, OMB, under the direction of the Federal CIO, established FDCCI in February 2010. This initiative's four high-level goals are to

- promote the use of "green IT"[7] by reducing the overall energy and real estate footprint of government data centers;
- reduce the cost of data center hardware, software, and operations;
- increase the overall IT security posture of the government; and
- shift IT investments to more efficient computing platforms and technologies.

As part of FDCCI, OMB required the 24 agencies to identify a data center consolidation program manager to lead the agency's consolidation efforts. In addition, agencies were required to submit an asset inventory baseline and other documents that would result in a plan for consolidating their data centers. The asset inventory baseline was to contain detailed information on each data center and identify the consolidation approach to be taken for each one. It would serve as the foundation for developing the final data center consolidation plan. The data center consolidation plan would serve as a technical road map and approach for achieving the targets for infrastructure utilization, energy efficiency, and cost efficiency and was to be incorporated into the agency's fiscal year 2012 budget.

In October 2010, OMB reported that all of the agencies had submitted an inventory and plan. In addition, in a series of memorandums, OMB described plans to monitor agencies' consolidation activities on an ongoing basis. Starting in fiscal year 2011, OMB required agencies to provide an updated data center asset inventory at the end of every third quarter and an updated consolidation plan (including any missing elements) at the end of every fourth quarter. Further, starting in fiscal year 2012, OMB required agencies to provide a consolidation progress report at the end of every quarter. This progress information has subsequently been made available on the federal website dedicated to providing the public with access to datasets developed by federal agencies, http://data.gov.

Pursuant to requirements of the Government Performance and Results Act Modernization Act of 2010 (GPRAMA),[8] in February 2012, OMB designated data center consolidation as 1 of its 14 priority goals (now known as cross-agency priority goals) because of its importance to improving management across the federal government. These goals are designed to cover areas where increased cross-agency collaboration is needed to improve progress towards the achievement of goals shared by multiple contributing agencies. In March 2014, OMB announced the creation of a new set of goals in its submission of the President's fiscal year 2015 budget, which did not include data center consolidation. According to OMB, although the updated set of goals did not include the data center consolidation goal because it had reached the end of its goal cycle time frame under GPRAMA, the effort will remain an administration priority.

While OMB is primarily responsible for FDCCI, the agency designated the Federal CIO Council—the principal interagency forum to improve IT-related practices across the federal government—to lead the effort. In addition, OMB originally identified two additional organizations to assist in managing and overseeing the initiative:

- The GSA FDCCI Program Management Office to support OMB in planning, execution, management, and communications.

- The Task Force is comprised of the data center consolidation program managers from each agency. According to its charter, the Task Force is critical to supporting collaboration across agencies, including identifying and disseminating key information, solutions, and processes that will help agencies in their consolidation efforts.

However, in December 2013, GSA and Task Force officials stated that the GSA's Program Management Office would no longer be supporting FDCCI and its responsibilities were being transitioned to OMB and the Task Force.

With an Expanded Definition, OMB's Inventory of Federal Data Centers Has Grown

OMB has used two different definitions for a data center throughout the life of FDCCI. In 2010, OMB defined a "data center" as any room used for the purpose of processing or storing data that is larger than 500 square feet, is used for processing or storing data, and meets stringent availability requirements.[9] While agencies included other facilities classified as a "server room" (typically smaller than 500 square feet) and "server closet" (typically smaller than 200 square feet) in their inventories, these facilities were not included in OMB's final tally of data centers. However, in October 2011, the Federal CIO expanded the definition to include a facility of any size. OMB further clarified its definition in March 2012, as follows:

> "...a data center is...a closet, room, floor or building for the storage, management, and dissemination of data and information and [used to house] computer systems and associated components, such as database, application, and storage systems and data stores [excluding facilities exclusively devoted to communications and network equipment (e.g., telephone exchanges and telecommunications rooms)]. A data center generally includes redundant or backup power supplies, redundant data communications connections, environmental controls...and special security devices housed in leased, owned, collocated, or stand-alone facilities."[10]

Under the first definition, OMB identified 2,094 data centers in July 2010. Using the new definition from October 2011, OMB estimated that there were a total of 3,133 federal data centers in December 2011, and its goal was to consolidate approximately 40 percent, or 1,253 data centers, for a savings of approximately $3 billion by the end of 2015.

Since 2011, the number of federal data centers reported by agencies has continued to grow. In July 2013, we testified[11] that 22 of the 24 FDCCI agencies had collectively reported 6,836 data centers in their inventories—an increase of about 3,700 compared to OMB's previous estimate from December 2011. According to the Federal CIO, the increase in data centers was primarily due to the expanded definition of a data center and improved inventory reporting by the agencies.

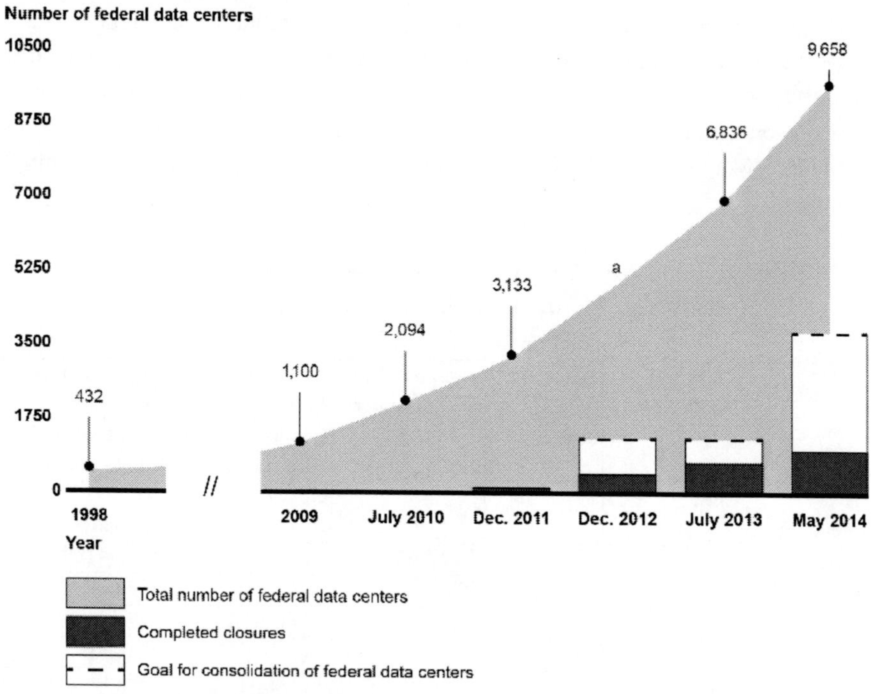

Source: GAO analysis of OMB and agency data. | GAO-14-713.

[a]OMB did not publically report the total number of data centers in 2012. OMB also expanded its definition of a data center in March 2012.

Figure 1. Total Number of Reported Federal Data Centers and Closures, as of May 2014.

More recently, our analysis of agencies' May 2014 data center inventories indicated that agencies collectively reported a total of 9,658 data centers. Of the total reported data centers, 242 were reported by agencies as "core" data centers—meaning that they are primary consolidation points for agency enterprise IT services and not planned for closure, while the remaining 9,416 were reported as "non-core."[12] OMB's March 2013 memorandum states that the goal is for agencies to close 40 percent of the total non-core data centers, or 3,766 data centers based on the May 2014 inventory data, by the end of fiscal year 2015.

Since 2011, agencies have reported their data center closures and planned closures on http://data.gov. As of May 2014, agencies collectively reported that they had closed a total of 976 data centers, and were planning to close an additional 2,689 data centers—for a total of 3,655—by the end of September 2015. See figure 1 for a summary of the total number of the federal data centers reported in agencies' inventories and closures as reported by agencies on http://data.gov over time, and table 1 for a depiction of the total number of data centers (including a breakdown of core and non-core centers) reported in agencies' May 2014 inventory submissions, and reported and planned closures.

Table 1. Total Number of Core and Non-core Data Centers and Completed and Planned Closures by Agency, as of May 2014

Agency	Core data centers	Non-core data centers	Total number of data centers	Closures through May 2014 (percent of non-core centers closed)	Total planned for closure (percent of non-core centers closed)[a]
Agriculture	4	2,273	2,277	41 (2%)	2,254 (99%)
Commerce	32	327	359	66 (20%)	79 (24%)
Defense	11	2,297	2,308	374 (16%)	939 (41%)
Education	3	2	5	0 (0%)	2 (100%)
Energy	5	52	57	7 (13%)	19 (37%)
HHS	27	199	226	52 (26%)	67 (34%)
DHS	3	102	105	26 (25%)	56 (55%)
HUD	1	1	2	0 (0%)	0 (0%)
Interior	6	410	416	71 (17%)	133 (32%)
Justice	3	107	110	53 (50%)	66 (62%)
Labor	9	84	93	8 (10%)	17 (20%)
State	4	386	390	5 (1%)	9 (2%)
Transportation	16	517	533	42 (8%)	171 (33%)
Treasury	4	2,133	2,137	102 (5%)	111 (5%)

Agency	Core data centers	Non-core data centers	Total number of data centers	Closures through May 2014 (percent of non-core centers closed)	Total planned for closure (percent of non-core centers closed)a
VA	87	257	344	15 (6%)	23 (9%)
EPA	4	77	81	19 (25%)	29 (38%)
GSA	4	119	123	60 (50%)	74 (62%)
NASA	11	48	59	25 (52%)	38 (79%)
NSF	0	2	2	1 (50%)	1 (50%)
NRC	1	8	9	0 (0%)	3 (38%)
OPM	4	0	4	0 (0%)	0 (0%)
SBA	0	4	4	0 (0%	2 (50%)
SSA	2	0	2	0 (0%)	0 (0%)
USAID	1	11	12	2 (18%)	3 (27%)
Totals	242	9,416	9,658	969 (10%)	4,096 (44%)

Source: GAO analysis of agency data. | GAO-14-713

Note: HHS—Department of Health and Human Services; DHS—Department of Homeland Security; HUD—Department of Housing and Urban Development; VA—Department of Veterans Affairs; EPA— Environmental Protection Agency; GSA—General Services Administration; NASA—National Aeronautics and Space Administration; NSF—National Science Foundation; NRC—Nuclear Regulatory Commission; OPM—Office of Personnel Management; SBA—Small Business Administration; SSA—Social Security Administration; USAID—U.S. Agency for International Development.

[a]Totals include data centers planned for closure beyond fiscal year 2015.

OMB Integrated FDCCI with Its PortfolioStat Initiative

In March 2012, OMB launched the PortfolioStat initiative, which requires agencies to conduct an annual agency-wide IT portfolio review to, among other things, reduce commodity IT[13] spending and demonstrate how its IT investments align with the agency's mission and business functions.[14] PortfolioStat is designed to assist agencies in assessing the current maturity of their IT portfolio management process, make decisions on eliminating duplication, and move to shared solutions in order to maximize the return on IT investments across the portfolio.

In September 2012, the Federal CIO wrote in an e-mail to agencies that OMB was planning to integrate FDCCI with the PortfolioStat initiative to allow agencies to focus on an enterprise-wide approach to address all commodity IT, including data centers, in an integrated, comprehensive plan and that agencies should continue to focus on optimizing those data centers that are essential to delivering taxpayer services, while continuing to close those that are duplicative. In addition, the e-mail directed agencies to delay submitting their October 1, 2012 submissions of updated consolidation plans until further guidance could be provided. However, agencies were still to report quarterly updates on their data center closures.

In March 2013, OMB issued a memorandum documenting the integration of FDCCI with PortfolioStat.[15] Among other things, the memorandum discussed OMB's efforts to further the PortfolioStat initiative by incorporating several changes, such as consolidating previously collected IT-related plans, reports, and data submissions. The guidance also stated that, to more effectively measure the efficiency of an agency's data center assets, agencies would also be measured by the extent to which their data centers are optimized for total cost of ownership by incorporating metrics for data center energy, facility, labor, and storage, among other things. OMB indicated in its memorandum that these metrics would be developed by the Task Force.

This March 2013 memorandum also established new agency reporting requirements and related time frames. Specifically, agencies were no longer required to submit the data center consolidation plans previously required under FDCCI. Rather, agencies were to submit information to OMB via three primary means—an information resources management strategic plan,[16] an enterprise road map,[17] and an integrated data collection channel.[18] In addition, agencies were still required to update their data center inventories yearly and report quarterly on http://data.gov regarding their consolidation progress.

More recently, in May 2014, OMB issued a memorandum updating its PortfolioStat guidance for fiscal year 2014.[19] As in past PortfolioStat guidance, the memorandum discussed the importance of PortfolioStat sessions—data-driven reviews of agency portfolio management between the Federal CIO, Agency Deputy Secretary, and other senior agency officials—as a means to continue to drive cost savings.

OMB's guidance also reinforced the need for agencies to continue to consolidate their non-core data centers while optimizing their core data centers using metrics established by the Task Force, and documented in OMB's memorandum. These metrics are discussed in more detail later in this report.

GAO Has Reported and Testified on Issues Related to Consolidating Data Centers

We have previously reported on OMB's efforts to consolidate federal data centers. In March 2011, we identified data center consolidation as one of the 81 areas within the federal government with opportunities to reduce potential duplication, overlap, and fragmentation. In this regard, we reported on the status of FDCCI and noted that data center consolidation made sense economically and was a way to achieve more efficient IT operations, but that challenges existed.[20] For example, agencies reported facing challenges in ensuring the accuracy of their inventories and plans, providing upfront funding for the consolidation effort before any cost savings accrue, and overcoming cultural resistance to such major organizational changes, among other things.

In July 2011, we issued a report on the status of FDCCI and found that only 1 of the 24 agencies had submitted a complete inventory and no agency had submitted complete plans. 21 Further, OMB had not required agencies to document the steps they had taken, if any, to verify the inventory data. We concluded that until these inventories and plans were complete, agencies would not be able to implement their consolidation activities and realize expected cost savings. Moreover, without an understanding of the validity of agencies' consolidation data, OMB could not be assured that agencies were providing a sound baseline for estimating consolidation savings and measuring progress against those goals. Accordingly, we made several recommendations to OMB, including that the Federal CIO require that agencies, when updating their data center inventory, state what actions were taken to verify the information in the inventory and to identify any associated limitations on the data, and to complete the missing elements in their inventories and consolidation plans.

OMB generally agreed with our report and has since taken actions to address our recommendations. For example, in July 2011, OMB required agency CIOs to submit a letter that identified steps taken to verify their data center inventory information and attest to the completeness of their consolidation plan. In addition, in March 2012, OMB required that all agencies complete all elements missing from their consolidation plans by the end of the fourth quarter of every fiscal year.

Additionally, in July 2012, we updated our review of FDCCI's status and found that, while agencies' 2011 inventories and plans had improved as compared to their 2010 submissions, only 3 agencies had submitted a complete inventory and only 1 agency had submitted a complete consolidation plan.[22] In addition, we noted that 3 agencies had submitted their inventory using an outdated format, in part, because OMB had not publicly posted its revised guidance. Notwithstanding these weaknesses, we noted that 19 agencies reported anticipating about $2.4 billion in cost savings between 2011 and 2015.

We also reported that none of five selected agencies had a master program schedule or cost-benefit analysis that was fully consistent with best practices. To assist agencies with their data center consolidation efforts, OMB had sponsored the development of a FDCCI total cost of ownership 23 model that was intended to help agencies refine their estimated costs for consolidation; however, agencies were not required to use the cost model as part of their cost estimating efforts. Accordingly, we reiterated our prior recommendation that agencies complete missing plan and inventory elements and made new recommendations to OMB to publically post guidance updates on the FDCCI website and to require agencies to use its cost model.

OMB generally agreed with our recommendations and has since taken steps to address them. More specifically, OMB posted its 2012 guidance for updating data center inventories and plans, as well as guidance for reporting consolidation progress, to the FDCCI public website. Further, the website has been updated to provide prior guidance documents and OMB memorandums. In addition, OMB's 2012 consolidation plan guidance required agencies to use the cost model as they developed their 2014 budget request.

More recently, in April 2013, we reported[24] on OMB and agencies' progress in consolidating federal data centers. Specifically, we reported that the 24 agencies participating in FDCCI had made progress by closing a total of 420 data centers by the end of December 2012. However, OMB had not measured agencies' progress against key performance measures, including its cost savings goal, or ensured that other key oversight responsibilities, such as approving agencies consolidation plans on the basis of their completeness, were being fully executed. We reported that OMB had not determined agencies' progress against its cost savings goal because, according to OMB staff, the agency had not determined a consistent and repeatable method for tracking cost savings and that the weaknesses in oversight were due, in part, to OMB not ensuring that assigned responsibilities were being executed. Accordingly, we recommended that OMB track and report on key performance measures, including cost savings, and improve the execution of important oversight responsibilities. OMB generally agreed with our recommendations and has since taken some initial actions to implement them, including tracking and reporting on data center consolidation cost savings on a quarterly basis.

Finally, between May 2013 and June 2014, we testified[25] on the status of FDCCI. Notably, in July 2013, we testified that, while agencies continued to make progress by closing an additional 64 data centers compared to the total number reported through the end of December 2012, the number of federal data centers had grown significantly since OMB's December 2011 estimate of approximately 3,133 data centers. Specifically, 22 of the 24 FDCCI agencies had collectively reported 6,836 data centers in their inventories—an increase of about 3,700 as compared to OMB's previous estimate from December 2011.[26] We concluded that it would be important for OMB to be transparent on agencies' progress against its performance metrics going forward.

Agencies Have Planned Substantial Consolidation Savings, but Reporting Can Be Improved

For FDCCI, OMB originally established a goal of achieving $3 billion in cost savings by the end of 2015. Pursuant to this goal, agencies have reported achieving more than a billion dollars in savings and avoidances through fiscal year 2013 and are planning a total of about $3.3 billion in savings and avoidances by the end of fiscal year 2015—an amount that is approximately $300 million higher than OMB's goal. Between fiscal years 2011 and 2017, agencies reported planning approximately $5.3 billion in total savings and avoidances. However, planned cost savings may be higher because six agencies with as many as 67 data center closures each have been limited in their abilities to fully report their savings. In addition, slightly more than half of agencies with planned cost savings are underreporting their fiscal years 2012 through 2015 figures to OMB by approximately $2.2 billion. While several agencies noted internal agency communication issues as the reasons for not reporting savings to OMB, other agencies were unable to provide a reason. Until agencies fully report their savings, the total planned cost savings and avoidances of $5.3 billion will be understated.

Agencies' Reported Savings Exceed More than a Billion Dollars through Fiscal Year 2013; Significant Additional Savings Planned through Fiscal Year 2017

Since launching FDCCI in 2010, achieving cost savings has been a primary goal of the initiative. As previously discussed, one of the original high-level objectives was to reduce the costs of data center hardware, software, and operations. OMB subsequently expanded on this goal and, in February 2012, stated that data center consolidation had the potential to achieve $3 billion dollars in savings by the end of 2015. Pursuant to these goals, OMB required agencies to describe year-by-year investments and cost savings in their 2010 and 2011 consolidation plans and, beginning in August 2013, has required agencies to identify and report all cost savings and avoidances[27] related to data center consolidation, among other areas, to OMB as part of a quarterly data collection process known as the integrated data collection.[28]

Most of the 24 agencies are achieving cost savings or avoidances from their data center consolidation efforts. Specifically, between fiscal years 2011 and 2013, 19 agencies collectively reported achieving an estimated $1.1 billion in cost savings and avoidances. Notably, Defense, the Department of Homeland Security (DHS), and the Department of the Treasury (Treasury) account for approximately $850 million (or 74 percent) of the reported estimated savings through fiscal year 2013. The remaining 5 agencies that did not report savings between fiscal years 2011 and 2013 cited varied reasons for not being able to do so, which included difficulties in determining baseline data center costs, upfront costs that have exceeded savings to date, and a lack of electrical metering to determine power usage savings.

The methodologies used to calculate savings varied across the 19 agencies that reported estimated or actual savings and avoidances through fiscal year 2013; however, most of these agencies estimated their figures. Specifically, 3 agencies—the Department of Education (Education), EPA, and the National Science Foundation (NSF)—reported actual cost savings and avoidances, which they determined by calculating differences in executed budget or contract amounts over time. The remaining 16 agencies estimated their cost savings and avoidances.

Table 2. Agency-reported Data Center Consolidation Cost Savings and Avoidances (FY 2011 through FY 2013)

Dollars in millions (rounded)						
Agency	Data center closures reported on data.gov, as of May 2014	FY 2011 actual or estimated savings and avoidances	FY 2012 actual or estimated savings and avoidances	FY 2013 actual or estimated savings and avoidances	Total cost savings and avoidances[a]	Estimated oractual costsavings andavoidances
Agriculture	41	$0	$27.63	$43.67	$71.30	Estimated
Commerce	68	6.15	17.04	29.58	52.77	Estimated
Defense	374	11.57	19.16	104.84	135.57	Estimated
Education	0	0	.25	.24	.49	Actual
Energy	7	1.80	.20	1.18	3.18	Estimated
HHS	52	0	0	4.34	4.34	Estimated
DHS	26	0	43.19	93.11	136.30	Estimated
HUD	0	0	0	0	0	None reported
Interior	65	.12	3.76	8.96	12.84	Estimated
Justice	54	.29	2.26	3.73	6.28	Estimated
Labor	11	0	0	0	0	None reported
State	5	1.60	3.53	5.68	10.81	Estimated
Transportation	42	0	10.06	21.25	31.31	Estimated
Treasury[b]	102	170.23	112.19	295.24	577.66	Estimated
VA	15	0	5.17	6.37	11.54	Estimated
EPA[b]	19	.37	17.88	52.55	70.80	Actual
GSA	67	0	3.38	9.47	12.85	Estimated
NASA	25	.17	.47	.66	1.30	Estimated
NSF	1	0	1.18	2.50	3.68	Actual

Table 2. (Continued)

Dollars in millions (rounded)						
Agency	Data center closures reported on data.gov, as of May 2014	FY 2011 actual or estimated savings and avoidances	FY 2012 actual or estimated savings and avoidances	FY 2013 actual or estimated savings and avoidances	Total cost savings and avoidances[a]	Estimated oractual costsavings andavoidances
NRC	0	0	.09	0	.09	Estimated
OPM	0	0	.32	0	.32	Estimated
SBA	0	0	0	0	0	None reported
SSA	0	0	0	0	0	None reported
USAID	2	0	0	0	0	None reported
Totals	976	192.30	267.76	683.37	1,143.43	

Source: GAO analysis of agency and OMB data. | GAO-14-713.

Note: HHS—Department of Health and Human Services; DHS—Department of Homeland Security; HUD—Department of Housing and Urban Development; VA—Department of Veterans Affairs; EPA— Environmental Protection Agency; GSA—General Services Administration; NASA—National Aeronautics and Space Administration; NSF—National Science Foundation; NRC—Nuclear Regulatory Commission; OPM—Office of Personnel Management; SBA—Small Business Administration; SSA—Social Security Administration; USAID—U.S. Agency for International Development.

[a]These figures do not fully reflect the costs associated with agencies' data center consolidation efforts because many agencies faced challenges in determining these costs, as discussed later in this report.

[b]For noted agencies, data center consolidation savings and avoidances were reported in the context of their broader IT infrastructure modernization efforts because of difficulties in separating out data center consolidation-specific savings.

As examples, GSA estimated its savings using the department's total cost of ownership model; the Department of the Interior (Interior) used post-consolidation forms collected from its component bureaus and offices to estimate cost savings related to areas such as rent, utilities, and personnel after a consolidation activity was completed; and Treasury estimated savings resulting from reductions in the percentage of IT infrastructure investment spending as compared to total IT spending over time. Officials at these agencies stated that they were limited to reporting estimating savings because of challenges in determining actual savings, including the lack of electrical metering to calculate power usage savings, budget and accounting systems that are not structured to account for the costs of individual data centers, and difficulties in determining costs and savings when data centers are located in multipurpose facilities. These issues are discussed in more detail later in this report.

See table 2 for a listing of agencies' data center closures, cost savings and cost avoidances between fiscal years 2011 and 2013, and whether the agency savings are estimated.

As prescribed by OMB's initial guidance on data center consolidation, the 19 agencies that reported achieving cost savings and avoidances did so using a variety of approaches. While these approaches can be grouped into four key areas—decommissioning, consolidation, cloud computing, and virtualization—agencies generally employed, and achieved cost savings and avoidances using, multiple approaches at the same time. For example, NSF officials stated that in order to reduce the agency's dependence on onsite infrastructure, the agency has been focused on increasing virtualization and consolidation of servers and storage, while continuing to adopt cloud computing technologies. See table 3 for a description of the four approaches and key examples of agency-reported savings or avoidances in each.

In addition to savings through fiscal year 2013, our analysis of estimated future savings shows that, collectively, agencies are reporting that they expect to exceed OMB's cost savings goal by the end of fiscal year 2015 and continue to achieve significant savings in future years. Specifically, 21 agencies collectively reported planning a total of about $3.3 billion in savings and avoidances by the end of 2015—an amount that is approximately $300 million higher than OMB's original $3 billion goal. Further, through fiscal year 2017, these agencies collectively reported planning an additional $2.1 billion in cost savings and avoidances, for a total of approximately $5.3 billion. Five agencies—the Department of Agriculture (Agriculture), Defense, DHS, the Department of Transportation (Transportation), and Treasury—account for about $4.9 billion (or approximately 91 percent) of the total savings reported. See table 4 for a listing of agencies' total cost savings and cost avoidances between fiscal years 2011 and 2017.

Table 3. Consolidation Approaches and Key Examples of Agency-reported Cost Savings and Avoidances

Approach	Selected agencies and key examples of reported cost savings and avoidances
Decommissioning Reducing underutilized or redundant physical servers or entire data centers. Examples include moving to an outsourced data center or reducing the number of physical assets.	• **DHS**–$136.30 million in cost savings between FY 2012 and FY 2013 due primarily to the decommissioning of component agency physical servers and operations and migrating to DHS's enterprise data centers. • **Defense**– $67.07 million in estimated savings between FY 2011 and FY 2013 due tofacility closures resulting in eliminating staff and reducing the facility costs per square foot. • **VA**– $11.54 million in cost avoidances between FY 2012 and FY 2013 due to migrating portions of its Veterans Health Information System and Technology Architecture to the Defense Information System Agency's enterprise computing centers, versus utilizing commercially leased data centers.
Consolidation Combining workload onto fewer computers or concentrating data processing into fewer physical facilities can help to reduce the cost of data center hardware, software, and operations, in addition to real estate and energy costs.	• **Treasury**–$577.66 million in estimated avoidances between FY 2011 and FY 2013 due to reductions in the percentage of IT infrastructure spending compared to total IT spending due to consolidation efforts within its end-user, network, and server investments.

Approach	Selected agencies and key examples of reported cost savings and avoidances
	• **Agriculture**– $71.30 million in estimated savings and avoidances between FY 2012 and FY2013 from reduced hardware and software maintenance and support costs; hardware refresh costs; data center energy and operational costs; and personnel costs from its consolidation effort. • **EPA**– $10.00 million in cost savings in FY 2012 due to a reduction in shared services costs (e.g., e-mail and licenses) as a result of the agency's IT infrastructure consolidation and optimization efforts.
Cloud computing Cloud computing relies on Internet-based services and resources to provide computing services to customers. Examples include web-based e-mail applications and common business applications that are accessed online instead of through a local computer.	• **Commerce**–$18.30million in estimated cost avoidances between FY 2011 through FY 2013 at the Census Bureau as a result of its private cloud initiative. • **Education**– $.49 million in cost savings and avoidances between FY 2012 and FY 2013 due to reduced power consumption as a result of moving servers and other IT services to contractor-owned and operated facilities using a cloud-based infrastructure. • **OPM**– $.32 million in estimated savings in FY 2012 by moving systems and servers to a combination of private and public cloud solutions.
Virtualization Virtualization is a technology that allows multiple software-based virtual machines that have different operating systems, to run in isolation, side by side, on the same physical machine. Virtualization is often used as part of cloud computing.	• **Defense**–$68.51 million in estimated savings in FY 2013 from efficiencies achieved,in part, through virtualization and operating system reductions, among other related areas.

Table 3. (Continued)

Approach	Selected agencies and key examples of reported cost savings and avoidances
	• **State**– $9.21 million in estimated cost avoidances between FY 2012 and FY 2013 due to the agency's virtualization effort, which enabled it to avoid costs associated with maintaining physical servers (e.g., hardware, power, and cooling). • **NSF**– $1.18 million in cost avoidances in FY 2012 due to the agency's server virtualization effort, which avoided costs related to maintenance and replacement of more than 100 legacy servers.

Key: FY = fiscal year.

Source: GAO analysis of agency data. | GAO-14-713.

Note: DHS—Department of Homeland Security; VA—Department of Veterans Affairs; EPA—Environmental Protection Agency; OPM—Office of Personnel Management; NSF—National Science Foundation.

Table 4. Agency-reported Total Data Center Consolidation Cost Savings and Avoidances (FY 2011 through FY 2017)

Dollars in millions (rounded)						
	FY 2011 through FY 2013	Planned cost savings and avoidances estimated by agencies				
Agency	actual and estimated cost savings and avoidances	FY 2014	FY 2015	FY 2016	FY 2017	Totals[a,b]
Agriculture	$71.30	$71.14	$101.73	n.d.	n.d.	$244.17
Commerce	52.77	22.25	8.09	1.98	1.49	86.58
Defense[c]	135.57	144.75	415.75	801.56	1,120.69	2,618.32
Education	.49	.24	.24	.24	n.d.	1.21
Energy	3.18	.57	.57	11.75	8.59	24.66
HHS	4.34	8.97	12.11	n.d.	n.d.	25.42
DHS	136.30	53.58	4.70	4.86	6.49	205.93
HUD	0	n.d.	n.d.	n.d.	n.d.	0
Interior	12.84	27.27	44.43	n.d.	n.d.	84.54
Justice	6.28	3.86	n.d.	n.d.	n.d.	10.14
Labor	0	.39	.85	n.d.	n.d.	1.24

Dollars in millions (rounded)						
	FY 2011 through FY 2013	Planned cost savings and avoidances estimated by agencies				
Agency	actual and estimated cost savings and avoidances	FY 2014	FY 2015	FY 2016	FY 2017	Totals[a,b]
State	10.81	7.63	11.60	0	0	30.04
Transportation	31.31	42.80	66.07	88.95	n.d.	229.13
Treasury	577.66	469.65	528.60	n.d.	n.d.	1,575.91
VA	11.54	6.37	6.37	6.37	6.37	37.02
EPA	70.80	.50	.65	.65	n.d.	72.60
GSA	12.85	15.30	20.65	n.d.	n.d.	48.80
NASA	1.30	.66	.66	.66	n.d.	3.28
NSF	3.68	3.07	.06	n.d.	n.d.	6.81
NRC	.09	n.d.	n.d.	n.d.	n.d.	.09
OPM	.32	3.08	n.d.	n.d.	n.d.	3.40
SBA	0	0	0	0	0	0
SSA	0	13.30	27.05	n.d.	n.d.	40.35
USAID	0	0	0	0	n.d.	0
Total	1,143.43	895.38	1,250.18	917.02	1,143.63	5,349.64

Key: FY = fiscal year; n.d. = no data.

Source: GAO analysis of agency data. | GAO-14-713.

Note: HHS—Department of Health and Human Services; DHS—Department of Homeland Security; HUD—Department of Housing and Urban Development; VA—Department of Veterans Affairs; EPA— Environmental Protection Agency; GSA—General Services Administration; NASA—National Aeronautics and Space Administration; NSF—National Science Foundation; NRC—Nuclear Regulatory Commission; OPM—Office of Personnel Management; SBA—Small Business Administration; SSA—Social Security Administration; USAID—U.S. Agency for International Development.

[a]These figures do not fully reflect the costs associated with agencies' data center consolidation efforts because many agencies faced challenges in determining these costs, as discussed later in this report.

[b]Three agencies—DHS, Energy, and VA—reported a total of approximately $62.07 million in additional savings between fiscal years 2018 and 2021; however, these savings are not reflected in the table because the remaining 21 agencies did not have data for these fiscal years.

[c]According to Defense officials, the department's planned cost savings figures are expected to vary over time as more data center assets are discovered, component agency plans mature, and estimating techniques continue to improve.

The extent of cost savings and avoidances being reported by agencies beyond fiscal year 2015 highlights the importance of OMB continuing to track and report on such savings beyond the time frame of its initial goal. Further, with many agencies having not yet reported on their planned savings, the savings beyond fiscal year 2015 may be higher than previously discussed. In this regard, we have previously recommended that OMB extend the horizon for realizing cost savings from FDCCI, as doing so could provide OMB and FDCCI stakeholders with input and information on the benefits of consolidation beyond OMB's initial goal.[29] OMB neither agreed nor disagreed with our recommendation but stated that, as the FDCCI and PortfolioStat initiatives proceed and continue to generate savings, OMB would consider whether updates to the current time frame are appropriate.

Savings May Be Higher than Current Amounts due to Underreporting of Planned Savings by Many Agencies

As previously mentioned, OMB's March 2013 memorandum[30] identified the requirements for reporting cost savings from data center consolidation. Specifically, the memorandum stated that agencies are required to report their data center consolidation cost savings and avoidances, among other areas, to OMB as part of a quarterly integrated data collection process. OMB's May 2014 memorandum[31] reiterated the requirements for integrated data collection submissions. Agencies can currently input cost savings and avoidances for fiscal years 2012 through 2015 into the web-based portal used to submit their integrated data collection submissions. Finally, standards for internal control emphasize the need for federal agencies to establish plans to help ensure goals and objectives can be met, including compliance with applicable laws and regulations.[32]

Although agencies are already collectively reporting approximately $5.3 billion in planned cost savings and avoidances from their consolidation efforts, these savings may be higher because 6 of the 24 agencies, claiming between 11 and 67 data center closures each, have been limited in their abilities to report savings. For example, although Interior reported closing 65 data centers as of May 2014, the agency cited significant challenges in obtaining costs and related savings information from its component agencies. In addition, the National Aeronautics and Space Administration (NASA) reported that, as of May 2014, it had closed 25 data centers; however, while the agency has been able to report $1.3 million in savings through fiscal year 2013, agency officials stated that NASA has been otherwise limited in its ability to identify cost savings and avoidances because of the agency's complex organizational structure, which includes multiple centers with multiple missions and multiple IT contractors utilizing data centers within multipurpose facilities. Similar challenges were also identified by other agencies, as discussed later in this report. Table 5 shows the agencies with limited or no savings relative to their consolidation efforts and their reasons for not being able to fully report savings.

Table 5. Agencies with Substantial Consolidation Efforts but Limited or No Savings Reported

Dollars in millions (rounded)			
Agency	Data center closures reported on data.gov, as of May 2014	Agency-reported estimated savings (FY 2011 through FY 2013)	Reason(s) for limited or no savings or avoidances reported
HHS	52	$4.34	HHS officials stated that significant savings have likely been realized from the closure of the agency's data centers, but the agency lacks the data needed to identify and document cost savings. Officials added that the CIO is developing a plan that is expected to address the challenges associated with the identification and documentation of cost savings; however, no time frame for completion of this plan has been established.
Interior	65	12.84	While Interior has developed a process to collect cost savings information from itscomponents, officials stated that individual bureaus and offices often do not have the detailed information to report on data center-specific savings because they donot have complete information about their facility costs (including power usage) and therefore cannot determine the facility cost savings.
Justice	54	6.28	Justice officials stated that that the department's decentralized organizational structure and culture have made it challenging to implement the data center consolidation initiative, but that more detailed plans to more aggressively consolidate and optimize IT services are being developed as the

Table 5. (Continued)

Dollars in millions (rounded)			
Agency	Data center closures reported on data.gov, as of May 2014	Agency-reported estimated savings (FY 2011 through FY 2013)	Reason(s) for limited or no savings or avoidances reported
			department collaboratively explores opportunities with its component agencies. However, no time frame has been established for completion of these plans.
Labor	11	0	Labor officials stated that the department's primary challenge in determining and measuring cost savings stems from issues in developing a baseline of the costs of IT services from which to calculate savings, but also noted that there is a lag between the time data centers are closed and when cost reductions can be realized. Officials added that consolidating and relocating systems and data centers to the department's enterprise data center is expected to provide the department with the capability to better measure data center costs; however, officials were unsure when the department would be able to determine cost savings.
GSA	67	12.85	GSA officials stated that, while the agency has had success in improving the quality of its data center inventory, it has been challenged in determining data center specific costs, cost savings, and cost avoidances. Officials stated that this is partly due to its decentralized organizational structure where data center costs (e.g., rents, leases, personnel, equipment repair, and replacement and service contracts) are distributed across 11 regions and six component agencies and their subordinate organizations.
NASA	25	1.30	NASA officials stated that the agency has been unable to capture actual cost savings and avoidances for its data center consolidation effort because of variouschallenges, including the

Agency	Data center closures reported on data.gov, as of May 2014	Agency-reported estimated savings (FY 2011 through FY 2013)	Reason(s) for limited or no savings or avoidances reported
			agency's complex organizational structure which includes multiple centers with multiple missions and multiple IT contractors utilizing data centers within multipurpose facilities—all of which make determining savings extremely complex and impractical. Officials noted that the agency has focused primarily on closing data centers and improving server densities at the agency's core data centers.

Key: FY = fiscal year.

Source: GAO analysis of agency data and interviews, and OMB data. | GAO-14-713.

Note: HHS—Department of Health and Human Services; GSA—General Services Administration; NASA—National Aeronautics and Space Administration.

Considering that cost savings is one of OMB's original high-level goals of FDCCI and reporting such savings is currently required on a quarterly basis, OMB has a responsibility for ensuring that agencies are identifying the full extent of cost savings from their consolidation efforts. Further, as previously mentioned, OMB's PortfolioStat guidance requires yearly review sessions of agency portfolio management (including data center consolidation) with the Federal CIO and senior agency officials and notes that these reviews are critical to driving cost savings.[33] We previously found[34] that all agencies held PortfolioStat sessions with OMB in fiscal year 2012. In addition, agencies were required to hold sessions again in 2013.[35] However, after 2 years of PortfolioStat sessions, the six agencies identified in the table have been limited in their ability to report savings from their data center consolidation efforts.

In addition, slightly more than half of the agencies with cost savings and avoidances did not fully report them to OMB—a requirement of OMB's quarterly integrated data collection process. Specifically, of the 21 agencies with actual and estimated fiscal years 2012 through 2015 cost savings and avoidances, 10 agencies fully reported their savings and avoidances to OMB through the integrated data collection process, 8 agencies partially reported this information, and 3 agencies did not report it. [36] As a result, agencies collectively reported savings for fiscal years 2012 through 2015 of approximately $3.1 billion to us, as compared to only about $876 million that agencies reported to OMB, meaning that the savings have been underreported to OMB by approximately $2.2 billion. See table 6 for a listing of agencies and a comparison of their data center consolidation savings as reported to GAO and through OMB's integrated data collection process.

Table 6. Comparison of Agency Consolidation Savings and Avoidances Reported to GAO against Agency Integrated Data Collection Submissions (as of May 2014)

Dollars in millions (rounded)			
	Cost savings and avoidances (FY 2012 through FY 2015)		
Agency	Reported to GAO	Reported to OMB via the integrated data collection process[a]	Were savings and avoidances reported to OMB?
Agriculture	$244.17	$71.20	Partially
Commerce	76.96	71.59	Partially
Defense	684.50	268.75	Partially
Education	.97	.97	Yes
Energy	2.52	1.19	Partially
HHS	25.42	28.66	Yes
DHS	194.58	194.58	Yes
HUD	0	0	N/A
Interior	84.42	13.59	Partially
Justice	9.85	9.85	Yes
Labor	1.24	1.24	Yes
State	28.44	28.44	Yes
Transportation	140.18	7.36	Partially
Treasury	1,405.68	12.01	Partially
VA	24.28	0	No
EPA	71.58	70.93	Partially
GSA	48.80	48.80	Yes
NASA	2.45	0	No
NSF	6.81	6.81	Yes
NRC	.09	.09	Yes
OPM	3.40	0	No
SBA	0	0	N/A
SSA	40.35	40.35	Yes
USAID	0	0	N/A
Total	3,096.69	876.41	

Key: FY = fiscal year; N/A = Not applicable. Agency did not report any cost savings or avoidances.

Source: GAO analysis of agency data. | GAO-14-713.

Note: HHS—Department of Health and Human Services; DHS—Department of Homeland Security; HUD—Department of Housing and Urban Development;

VA—Department of Veterans Affairs; EPA— Environmental Protection Agency; GSA—General Services Administration; NASA—National Aeronautics and Space Administration; NSF—National Science Foundation; NRC—Nuclear Regulatory Commission; OPM—Office of Personnel Management; SBA—Small Business Administration; SSA—Social Security Administration; USAID—U.S. Agency for International Development.

[a]These figures do not reflect the implementation costs associated with agencies' data center consolidation efforts because many agencies did not report these costs to OMB.

While several agencies noted internal agency communication issues as a reason that their savings and avoidances were not fully reported, other agencies were not able to provide a reason. These shortcomings in agency reporting have resulted in OMB not being able to fully report agencies' data center consolidation cost savings and avoidances in its quarterly reports to Congress on the status of federal IT reform efforts, in accordance with its responsibilities as set forth in law. For example, OMB's May 2014 report to Congress[37] noted total fiscal years 2012 and 2013 data center consolidation cost savings and avoidances of slightly less than $329 million, as compared to the approximately $951 million that agencies reported to us that they achieved over that same time period—a difference of approximately $622 million.

Until OMB assists those agencies with limited or no cost savings reported, agencies may not be able to identify the full extent of savings from their consolidation efforts and the total planned cost savings and avoidances of approximately $5.3 billion will be understated. Further, until agencies fully report their cost savings and avoidances to OMB, Congress may be limited in its ability to oversee agencies' progress against key initiative goals.

AGENCIES REPORTED SUCCESSES AND CHALLENGES IN ACHIEVING COST SAVINGS

Nearly all agencies reported experiencing differing types of success in achieving cost savings. Specifically, 22 of the 24 agencies identified a total of 21 types of success,[38] while the remaining 2 agencies—the Department of Housing and Urban Development (HUD) and the Small Business Administration (SBA)—did not identify any. Five types of successes were identified by five agencies or more, with the most-reported being identified by 22 agencies. Table 7 details the reported successes as well as the number of related agencies; the most common successes are further discussed after the table.

Table 7. Agency Consolidation Successes in Achieving Cost Savings

Successes	Numberof agencies
Focused on virtualization and cloud services as consolidation solutions	22
Reduced power consumption	7
Reduced facility costs (e.g., rent and maintenance)	6
Ensured a more comprehensive asset inventory	6
Standardized IT capabilities (e.g., hardware, software, and security architecture)	5
Provided data center services (e.g., cloud infrastructure and hosting services) to other agencies to decrease costs or increase revenues	2
Realized savings and efficiencies from the migration to enterprise data centers	2
Used data centers owned, leased, or operated by other agencies	2
Eliminated duplicative investments in IT hardware, software and support services	2
More efficiently delivered computing services	2
Instituted a culture of continuous process improvement to seek new, cost effective methods, tools, and solutions for data center migration	1
Improved internal agency coordination between the CIO and Chief Financial Officer	1
Implemented cultural changes (e.g., teleworking) to facilitate consolidation	1
Identified additional opportunities for consolidation through a space management assessment	1
Renegotiated shared service labor contracts	1
Increased CIO budget authority	1
Used energy savings performance contracts	1
Worked with component agencies to find consolidation opportunities	1
Increased granularity of infrastructure investments (i.e., end user, network, and server investments) to increase transparency and better identify savings	1
Improved data center consolidation-related planning	1
Implemented lessons learned and consolidation best practices, such as developing tools for identifying network, server, and storage utilization statistics	1

Source: GAO analysis of agency data and interviews with agency officials. | GAO-14-713.

Nearly All Agencies Reported That Virtualization and Cloud Services Have Produced Cost Savings

Twenty-two agencies reported that focusing on virtualization and cloud services have proven successful in achieving cost savings. Virtualization is a technology that allows multiple, software-based machines with different operating systems, to run in isolation, side by side, on the same physical machine. Cloud computing is a form of computing that relies on Internet-based services and resources to provide computing services to customers, while freeing them from the burden and costs of maintaining the underlying infrastructure. As previously mentioned, OMB suggests that agencies use a combination of approaches—two of which are virtualization and cloud computing—in their consolidation efforts. In 2012, we found that 9 agencies reported that focusing on virtualization and cloud computing had helped improve their consolidation efforts.[39]

As noted previously, Defense reported about $68.51 million in estimated savings in fiscal year 2013 from efficiencies achieved, in part, through virtualization and operating system reductions. Defense officials noted that the department's current goal is a 30 percent reduction in operating systems by the end of fiscal year 2017. In addition, the Department of State (State) reported $9.21 million in estimated cost avoidances between fiscal years 2012 and 2013 to OMB due to the department's virtualization effort, which enabled it to avoid costs associated with maintaining physical servers (e.g., hardware, power, and cooling).

As another example, NSF officials stated that virtualization had helped the agency reduce its server footprint by more than 100 servers in fiscal year 2012, resulting in related cost avoidances of $1.18 million. Officials noted that the reduction in servers reduced the labor required to support the servers, the funding needed for hardware maintenance renewals, and the costs to implement future hardware upgrades. Finally, in its quarterly report to OMB, Transportation stated that the department reduced one of its data center's floor space by 62 percent and the number of physical servers from 88 to 34 in fiscal year 2013 by leveraging virtualization solutions. According to the department, this led to reduced costs for operations and maintenance, as well as a number of other benefits, including enhanced security protection, scalability, and disaster recovery activities.

In addition, agencies also shared with us the advantages of moving their organizations to cloud services and the resulting cost savings. For example, EPA reported that it consolidated its e-mail services to its private cloud, reducing the number of e-mail servers from over 180 to 20 and standardizing its e-mail data and archive management practices.

According to the agency, this resulted in savings of $1 million in fiscal year 2012. Further, in its quarterly submission to OMB, GSA reported that it expects to save slightly more than $12 million over 4 years, when compared to the considered alternative, by switching its e-mail services to a cloud provider. Agriculture also reported that it uses cloud services to host most of its major applications, which resulted in increased server utilization and reduced operating costs, among other things. For example, the department reported that its cloud environments operated at average server utilization rates of 55 to 65 percent versus the 10 to 20 percent average utilization rates it typically found across its legacy server environments.

Many Agencies Reported Success in Reducing Data Center Power Consumption and Facility Costs to Achieve Savings

Seven agencies reported that reducing power consumption had proven successful in achieving cost savings. For example, NASA reported that its consolidation efforts at the Kennedy Space Center had eliminated 913 servers, which reduced power consumption by approximately three million kilowatt hours per year and resulted in estimated cost savings of $288,000 annually. In addition, Energy reported that it saved an estimated $130,000 annually due to reduced power consumption resulting from the consolidation of two of its data centers. Further, Education reported that by shutting down the air conditioning units in 25 local area network closets it was able to reduce power consumption and achieve savings of approximately $247,000 between fiscal years 2011 and 2012. The Department of Commerce (Commerce), Defense, NSF, and the Nuclear Regulatory Commission (NRC) also stated that reduced power consumption successfully resulted in cost savings.

Six agencies also reported that they had been successful in reducing their data center facility costs. For example, Defense reported that facility closures, with resulting reductions in staff and facility costs, had resulted in $67.07 million in estimated savings between fiscal years 2011 and 2013. Similarly, Energy reported that it avoided $7.3 million in facility costs related to operations and maintenance expenses by closing two data centers. Further, the Department of Health and Human Services (HHS) reported saving about $2.3 million from fiscal years 2011 to 2013 by reducing facility costs. This was due to rent and generator maintenance fees that no longer needed to be paid after a data center was closed in fiscal year 2011. Commerce reported almost $2 million in savings and avoidances related to reduced facility costs as a result of its consolidation effort. Finally, NASA reported that it was able to reduce facility costs through a reduction of slightly more than 28,000 square feet of floor space at its Kennedy Space Center, for estimated savings of about $247,000 annually.

Improved Asset Inventories Have Helped Agencies Better Achieve Savings

Six agencies reported that having a more comprehensive data center inventory led to cost savings. DHS officials stated that improved information in the department's data center inventory helped to better plan data center relocations. The department noted that, while this did not cut down on the cost of consolidation, it served to improve DHS's ability to project the actual costs of, and savings related to, data center migrations to its enterprise data centers. In addition, Defense officials stated that the department had been able to leverage authorities granted to the CIO in the National Defense Authorization Act for Fiscal Year 2012[40] to withhold funding from component organizations that do not submit accurate and up-to-date data center inventories on time to the CIO. Officials added that these authorities have significantly helped the department in its consolidation effort and in achieving cost savings. As another example, State reported that updates and changes to its data center inventory had resulted in a more complete and accurate picture of the department's data center environment. The department also reported using the updated totals for servers, floor space, and power consumption to calculate its cost avoidances. Commerce, NASA, and Transportation also reported benefits from an improved data center inventory.

Standardization of IT Services Improved Capability Delivery, Resulting in Cost Savings

Five agencies also reported success through the standardization of IT capabilities. For example, EPA reported that the agency had achieved $10 million in cost savings in fiscal year 2012 due to the standardization of IT services such as adopting agency-wide IT procurement, consolidating to an agency-wide help desk, optimizing its disaster recovery practices, and reducing software licenses through shared services. As another example, Defense indicated that standardization of hardware, software, and security architectures led to improved capability delivery and cyber security, and contributed to efficiency savings. Further, GSA reported that standardizing its enterprise document management solutions, simplifying its IT infrastructure, and improving information sharing to enable data-driven decision making had led to cost savings. In addition, the Departments of Veterans Affairs (VA) and Interior also reported successfully standardizing IT services to improve capability delivery and achieve cost savings.

The consolidation successes in achieving cost savings experienced by agencies indicate that they are making progress to realize the goals of FDCCI. Further, many of these reported accomplishments directly relate to the four approaches to consolidating data centers—decommissioning, consolidation, cloud computing, and virtualization—discussed earlier in this report, thereby demonstrating that OMB's consolidation road map continues to provide a realistic means by which agencies can achieve cost savings.

Agencies Reported That Efforts to Achieve Consolidation Cost Savings Face Challenges Similar to Those Previously Reported

In 2011 and 2012, we reported[41] on the broad challenges that agencies were facing during data center consolidations. These included FDCCIrelated, cultural, funding-related, operational, and technical challenges. In 2014, agencies reported that many of the same challenges still exist and impacted their ability to achieve cost savings through consolidation efforts. In addition, agencies identified many new challenges that were specific to achieving cost savings. As we found previously, some challenges are more common than others, with the most-reported challenge being faced by a total of eight agencies. One agency—HUD— did not report any challenges. Table 8 details the reported challenges and the numbers of agencies experiencing that challenge. The table is followed by a discussion of the most prevalent challenges.

Table 8. Agency Consolidation Challenges in Achieving Cost Savings

Challenge type	Challenge	Number of agencies
Operational (31)	Gathering data from component agencies or organizations (e.g., data center inventories and cost savings)	6
	Determining costs and realizing savings when data centers are located in shared, multipurpose facilities	5
	Determining baseline costs of existing data center facilities from which to calculate savings	4

Challenge type	Challenge	Number of agencies
	Realizing significant cost savings from closure of smaller data centers (i.e., server rooms or closets)	2
	Using OMB's total cost of ownership model for planning consolidation savings	2
	Consolidation costs of upgrading services and infrastructure have exceeded savings	1
	Lack of suitable government-wide acquisition vehicles for cloud solutions	1
	Increasing vendor costs offset savings experienced through consolidation	1
	Contractual obligations, such as number of end-users supported, preclude the realization of savings through consolidation until those obligations end	1
	Coordinating internal and external entities involved in facilities, data center, and IT planning and related activities	1
	Making renovations required to repurpose office space delays savings	1
	Achieving savings from data center migration activities	1
	Relocating already consolidated hardware has not yielded cost savings	1
	Lack of finalized consolidation strategies and plans limited the agency to focusing on consolidating smaller facilities, thus preventing significant cost savings	1
	Consolidation activities will not be fully implemented until fiscal year 2016	1
	Consolidation efforts started prior to the Federal Data Center Consolidation Initiative make it difficult to identify and quantify savings	1
	Increasing demand for services offsets savings from consolidation	1
Technical (14)	Lack of electricity metering to determine power usage information	8
	Increased telecommunication costs after relocating small data centers or applications	2
	Relocating to enterprise data centers revealed system deficiencies that required additional costs to address (i.e., lack of disaster recovery)	1

Table 8. (Continued)

Challenge type	Challenge	Number of agencies
	Need for significant systems engineering expertise and level of effort to take advantage of cost savings opportunities	1
	Physical hardware needs to be updated before savings from virtualizing legacy systems can be realized	1
	Readiness of systems, applications, and organizations to migrate to a shared infrastructure (i.e., enterprise data center)	1
Financial (14)	Obtaining the funding within their agency for consolidation efforts	8
	Structuring budget and accounting systems to account for individual data centers	6
Cultural (12)	Decentralized organizational structure was not geared toward consolidation	6
	Accepting cultural change that is part of consolidation	3
	Changing mission priorities	2
	Collaborating with other agencies to utilize excess capacity	1

Source: GAO analysis of agency data and interviews with agency officials. | GAO-14-713.

Operational Challenges

Agencies reported that the most significant operational challenges included difficulty in obtaining information (such as data center inventory and cost savings data) from component organizations and determining costs and realizing savings when data centers were located in shared, multipurpose facilities. Specifically, 6 agencies reported that obtaining consolidation-related data from component organizations as a challenge to achieving cost savings which is similar to, but not as prevalent as, the 10 agencies we found having difficulty providing good quality asset inventories in 2012. For example, Defense's Data Center Consolidation Lead noted that getting component organizations to report all of their data centers remains a challenge in achieving cost savings, particularly in the case of smaller, single-server data centers (e.g., research stations or computers that are only used by a few individuals and are often not reported until replacement or enhancement is needed). Additionally, Agriculture's Associate CIO for Data Center

Operations stated that it was often difficult to determine actual cost savings because the department's 32 component agencies did not track their total cost of IT, as portions are funded from many different sources versus being under the control of the component agency or office CIO (e.g., building rent and utilities, salaries, construction, etc.).

In addition, whereas we found in 2012 that one agency had difficulty with identifying and quantifying actual costs associated with data center facilities, we found that five agencies reported that it was difficult to determine costs and realized savings when data centers were located in shared, multipurpose facilities. For example, Energy reported that because several of its data centers were located in shared-use facilities, it was difficult for the department to determine the centers' total operating costs without an additional investment in advanced electricity metering. Energy also noted that it is difficult to determine the total cost savings and avoidances associated with the closure of these data centers until they are decommissioned and the vacated floor space is repurposed. EPA also reported that its data centers and server rooms were housed within mixed-use facilities, which generally cannot be discarded. Further, EPA expects that most former data center spaces will continue to provide local telecommunications and building access support services, which reduces potential substantive building operational cost reductions due to room decommissioning.

Technical Challenges

Agencies reported that the most significant technical challenges included a lack of electricity metering to determine power usage information and increased telecommunication costs after relocating small data centers or applications. The lack of electricity metering is similar to the difficulty we previously found for 15 agencies in 2012 with obtaining power usage information. Our current work found that 8 agencies reported that a lack of electricity metering to determine power usage was a challenge. For example, the Department of Labor (Labor) reported that a lack of electricity metering at many data centers prevented the department from accurately reporting energy savings attributed to the consolidation effort. Labor officials added that it was difficult to perform power usage efficiency calculations because the data to feed the calculations were not available.

As other examples, Transportation reported that its smaller data centers were operated in GSA-owned buildings which did not have electricity metering for the data center spaces. Transportation also noted that many of these spaces also contain telecommunications equipment which would remain after the data center equipment is relocated or decommissioned, which would mean the closures are not expected to produce significant savings. Further, NASA reported that it had encountered difficulties in metering its older, less-efficient facilities and that the modifications needed to make the facilities more efficient would require a significant amount of resources and yield a low return on investment. In addition, those modifications would adversely impact current operations due to the requisite power outages to install metering equipment. Commerce, Defense, Interior, NSF, and the Social Security Administration (SSA) also reported a lack of electricity metering as a challenge.

Regarding increased telecommunication costs, Interior and Transportation both reported this area as a challenge. Interior noted that the higher telecommunication premiums realized from its effort often offset the savings from consolidating a large number of small and closet-sized data centers. Transportation officials also stated that that the relocation of locally run applications to a consolidated data center may lead to increased telecommunications costs.

Financial Challenges

Agencies reported two financial challenges related to obtaining the funding required within their agency for consolidation efforts, as well as budget and accounting system issues that impacted their ability to achieve cost savings. In 2012, we found that nine agencies considered obtaining the funding required for consolidation and migration efforts to be a challenge. In 2014, eight agencies identified this challenge. For example, VA reported that the investment funding for all phases of its consolidation plan has not been available from the department as initially scheduled and, as a result has had to evolve its plan to address the risk of continued investment funding shortfalls so that it can continue to make progress towards its consolidation goals. In addition, SBA officials stated that a lack of funding allocated to implementing its data center consolidation strategy has been the primary challenge in achieving data center consolidation cost savings. Officials added that, in light of this challenge, the agency continues to examine federal cloud and GSA e-mail-as-a-service offerings, and initiated a request to the SBA investment governance process and a fiscal year 2015 request to pilot and migrate agency e-mail to a GSA vendor-managed cloud provider.

In addition, six agencies reported having budget and accounting systems that were not structured to account for individual data centers. For example, Energy officials stated that data centers have generally operated from separate facility and IT operations budgets and specific facility cost elements have not been tracked. In addition, officials added that different budgets are used to support different data centers, resulting in a lack of a consolidated budget for data centers, and has made documenting costs and related savings difficult. In addition, VA officials stated that IT costs often encompass multiple data centers and user facilities, making it challenging to parse the costs to the individual data centers and determine related savings.

Cultural Challenges

Agencies reported that the most significant cultural challenges included having a decentralized organizational structure that was not geared toward consolidation and accepting the cultural changes that were part of consolidation. In 2012, we found that two agencies encountered cultural challenges related to having a decentralized organization structure and five agencies had difficulty accepting cultural change as part of the consolidation effort. Our current work showed six agencies encountered cultural challenges related to having a decentralized organization structure. For example, GSA reported that its foremost challenge was that its data center costs and expenses were distributed across a federated organization. The agency indicated that the costs for rents; leases; personnel; and equipment repair, replacement, and service contracts were distributed across 11 regions, six components, and their subordinate organizations. Further, the Department of Justice (Justice) reported that its federated organizational structure had made it especially challenging to implement enterprise-wide initiatives such as data center consolidation. Officials noted that this was due, in part, to the need to build consensus for, plan, and then implement the consolidation changes, which does not happen quickly in a decentralized environment.

In addition, three agencies stated that accepting the cultural changes required to implement their consolidation efforts impacted their ability to achieve cost savings. For example, Justice also noted that its federated environment made it difficult for people to accept the cultural changes that are part of consolidation. Further, officials from Agriculture reported the challenge of accepting culture change as it encountered resistance to consolidation-related changes, including the use of cloud computing, from component agency personnel.

In any significant IT initiative, it is important that both successes and challenges be highlighted. In the case of FDCCI, a success highlights approaches and strategies that have helped agencies to achieve cost savings and fulfill the intent of the initiative. Conversely, a challenge identifies an area that was impacting an agency's ability to achieve cost savings and meet the intent of this government-wide effort. In light of how closely the successes and challenges reported by agencies relate to achieving cost savings—a key OMB goal for FDCCI—it will be important for OMB to continue to provide leadership and guidance to the initiative. This includes, as we have previously recommended, utilizing the Task Force—the primary organization responsible for supporting collaboration and knowledge transfer across the FDCCI agencies—to monitor and assist with agencies' consolidation efforts.[42]

DATA CENTER OPTIMIZATION METRICS AND RELATED TARGETS ARE LARGELY ESTABLISHED, BUT KEY AREA NOT ADDRESSED

Leading practices[43] have established the need for initiatives to develop performance measures to gauge progress. According to government and industry leading practices, performance measures should be measurable, outcome-oriented (i.e., identify targets for improving performance), and actively tracked and reported. In accordance with these principles, OMB's March 2013 memorandum[44] directed the Task Force to develop data center metrics for energy, facility, labor, storage, virtualization and cost per operating system to enable the measurement of the extent to which federal agency core data centers are optimized for total cost of ownership.

In May 2014, OMB released a set of 11 data center consolidation optimization metrics established by the Task Force. [45] These metrics address all of the categories defined in the March 2013 memorandum. In addition, related targets to be achieved by the end of fiscal year 2015 have been established for all the metrics except for the cost-peroperating-system metric, which provides for measuring progress on optimizing data center costs. According to a Task Force official, current data center inventory data (already required to be submitted by agencies on at least a yearly basis) will be used to calculate agencies' progress using the metrics and related targets. See table 9 for a list of the metrics, including the related category, a brief description, and the established target for each metric.

Table 9. Core Data Center Optimization Metrics and Targets

Metric	Metric category	Description	Target value (to be achieved by the end of FY 2015)
Power usage effectiveness	Energy	The amount of total power consumed at a facility divided by the total amount of IT power consumed.	1.5 or lower
Cost per operating system per hour	Cost per operating system	The total costs of a data center divided by the number of operating systems, figured for an hourly cost basis.	Not yet established [a]
Full-time equivalent ratio	Labor	The total number of servers divided by the total number of data center personnel (government and contract employees).	At least 25 servers per full-time equivalent
Facility utilization	Facility	The total number of server racks multiplied by 30 square feet and then divided by the total square feet reported in the data center.	At least 80 percent
Storage utilization	Storage	The total storage used divided by the total storage available.	75 percent for in-house storage utilization and/or 80 percent for cloud computing /outsourced facilities
Core to non-core physical server ratio	Facility	The number of physical servers in core data centers vs. the number of physical servers in non-core data centers.	At least 65 percent
Core to non-core operating system ratio	Virtualization	The number of operating systems in core data centers vs. the number of operating systems in non-core data centers.	At least 65 percent
Virtualized operating systems	Virtualization	The number of virtualized operating systems divided by the total number of operating systems.	75 percent of operating systems virtualized

Table 9. (Continued)

Metric	Metric category	Description	Target value (to be achieved by the end of FY 2015)
Virtualization density	Virtualization	The number of virtual operating systems per virtual host.	10 operating systems per virtual host
Virtual hosts	Virtualization	The number of virtualized hosts divided by the total number of servers.	At least 20 percent
Virtualization optimization percent	Virtualization	Average of the preceding three metrics: virtualized operating systems, virtualization density, and virtual hosts.	Not applicable—average of the three metrics above

Source: GAO analysis of OMB and Task Force data. | GAO-14-713.
[a]According to OMB staff, this target is expected to be finalized in the fall of 2014.

According to OMB staff from the Office of E-Government and Information Technology, there have been challenges in reaching consensus on the cost-per-operating-system target. Specifically, the staff stated that the Task Force has had difficulty with developing a baseline for cloud computing costs that could be used to establish an appropriate target because private sector cloud providers are continually cutting the prices for their services. Development of the cost-per-operating-system target is expected to continue and OMB staff stated that the Task Force expects to finalize the target in the fall of 2014.

In addition, although low server utilization rates were a driving force cited by OMB in launching FDCCI, the new data center optimization metrics do not address this key issue. As previously mentioned, in 2009, OMB reported[46] that server utilization rates were as low as 5 percent across the federal government's servers. OMB subsequently required agencies to report on server utilization percentage as part of their 2011 and 2012 consolidation plans and included a suggested target of 60 to 70 percent server utilization in its 2011 and 2012 FDCCI consolidation plan guidance. OMB later eliminated the requirement for agencies to continue to update their consolidation plans, but indicated in its March 2013 memorandum[47] that it would continue tracking agencies' progress through other means, including the data center optimization metrics.

However, a metric for server utilization was not included in the final metrics established by the Task Force. According to an official from the GSA FDCCI Program Management Office that led initial efforts to establish the metrics, server utilization was not included as a metric for a variety of reasons, including that agencies have not traditionally collected the necessary data to be able to calculate server utilization, agencies do not have the server monitoring capabilities required to collect such data, and improvements in other areas of the metrics (such as virtualization) would likely result in higher server utilization. However, as previously mentioned, with server utilization a driving factor for FDCCI and measuring as low as 5 percent as recently as 2009, determining progress against this metric is critical to improving the efficiency, performance, and environmental footprint of federal data center activities.

Without an established target for one of its key cost metrics, the cost per operating system, OMB may not be getting complete information about agencies' progress in their data center optimization efforts and, therefore, may be lacking important insight that limits its ability to take corrective actions as needed. In addition, without a specific metric for server utilization, OMB may not be fully aware of agencies' progress on a key metric that was a driving force in launching FDCCI.

CONCLUSION

After slightly more than 4 years into FDCCI, agencies have begun to report significant savings from their consolidation efforts—most notably, Defense, DHS, and Treasury, which account for 74 percent of the reported savings to date. Furthermore, with approximately $3.3 billion in total planned savings being reported by agencies through fiscal year 2015, meeting OMB's savings goal is increasingly more likely and, if executed as planned, would represent a significant accomplishment for OMB and the FDCCI agencies. However, limited or no savings achieved at agencies with major consolidation efforts underway suggests that additional actions are necessary. OMB's and these agencies' continued efforts to address challenges and identify cost savings opportunities, through the use of such existing mechanisms as PortfolioStat sessions, will result in even more savings. Additionally, agencies' continued underreporting of consolidation savings will limit OMB's ability to accurately track agencies' progress and report to Congress, a point highlighted by the significant understatement of agency-reported savings—by approximately $622 million through fiscal year 2013—in OMB's recent congressional submission, and—by over $2.2 billion through fiscal year 2015—in agency data submissions to OMB.

As the federal consolidation effort has matured over the past few years, agencies have reported noteworthy successes in achieving cost savings—particularly in leveraging virtualization and cloud computing as a means to achieve such savings. These constructive experiences, which stem from OMB's recommended consolidation strategies, indicate that FDCCI is moving in the right direction. However, as agencies work toward achieving their cost savings goals, many continue to report challenges related to gathering the necessary technical information from which to calculate savings and funding the consolidation itself. While these challenges are consistent with those reported in the past, others, such as determining savings when data centers are located in multipurpose facilities, have become more prominent. Such a dynamic environment reinforces the need for agencies to remain in communication with OMB in order to facilitate knowledge sharing and transfer and for OMB to continue to provide leadership and guidance, as we have previously recommended.

OMB's May 2014 publication of the data center optimization metrics is a considerable step forward in helping OMB provide better oversight of agencies' efforts to optimize their core data centers. Furthermore, targets established for nearly all the metrics will provide agencies with clear and transparent goals to guide their data center optimization efforts. However, the continued absence of a metric for server utilization, despite OMB's previously-reported concerns about low average utilization rates, represents a missed opportunity to track agencies' progress on this metric. In the absence of such a metric, OMB will be challenged in demonstrating agencies' improvement in an area that was a driving force in starting FDCCI and which is critical to improving the efficiency, performance, and environmental footprint of federal data center activities.

Recommendations for Executive Action

To better ensure that FDCCI improves governmental efficiency and achieves cost savings, we are making two recommendations to OMB. We recommend that the Director of OMB direct the Federal CIO to:

- utilize the existing PortfolioStat review sessions to assist HHS, Interior, Justice, Labor, GSA, and NASA in identifying data center consolidation cost savings opportunities; and
- as part of any future evaluation of the data center optimization metrics, develop and implement a metric for server utilization.

We also recommend that the Secretaries of HHS, the Interior, Justice, and Labor, and the Administrators of GSA and NASA complete action plans for addressing their challenges in reporting cost savings, as discussed in this report.

Finally, we recommend that the Secretaries of Agriculture, Commerce, Defense, Energy, the Interior, Transportation, the Treasury, and VA; the Administrators of EPA and NASA; and the Director of the Office of Personnel Management direct responsible officials to report all data center consolidation cost savings and avoidances to OMB in accordance with established guidance.

AGENCY COMMENTS AND OUR EVALUATION

We received comments on a draft of our report from OMB, the 15 agencies to which we made recommendations, and the other 9 agencies mentioned in the report. Specifically, OMB and 12 agencies agreed with our recommendations, 1 agency did not state whether it agreed or disagreed, 1 agency had no comments, and 1 agency—NASA—agreed with one of our recommendations but partially agreed with the other. The other 9 agencies had no specific comments on our recommendations.

Multiple agencies also provided technical comments, which we incorporated as appropriate. Each of the agency's comments are discussed in more detail below.

- In comments provided by e-mail on July 30, 2014, a policy analyst from OMB's Office of E-Government and Information Technology stated that OMB agreed with the findings and recommendations of the report. OMB also provided technical comments, which we have incorporated as appropriate.
- In comments provided by e-mail, a liaison officer from Agriculture's Office of the CIO stated that the department agreed with the report's recommendation and noted steps planned to address the recommendation, including engaging with Agriculture agencies to

collect actual cost savings and avoidance information realized through their internal consolidation efforts. In addition, the department noted that the Office of the CIO is drafting a Cloud Computing Departmental Directive that, in addition to other requirements, is expected to standardize the process by which IT investments are evaluated for cloud services, including projected and actual cost savings and avoidances.

- In written comments, Commerce's Deputy Secretary stated that the department concurred with the general findings of the report as they applied to Commerce. The department did not state whether it agreed or disagreed with our recommendation, but noted that department would ensure that all savings and avoidances identified by its component bureaus are reported through OMB's integrated data collection.
- Our draft report provided to Defense for comment included a recommendation that the department complete an action plan for addressing their challenges in reporting cost savings. This was based on the department withdrawing its original savings figures—totaling approximately $4.7 billion between fiscal years 2011 through 2017—reported earlier in our review, and submitting revised figures using a new methodology that did not result in planned cost savings estimates beyond fiscal year 2014. Subsequently, Defense provided additional documentation of its planned savings between fiscal years 2015 and 2017, which resulted in an updated total planned cost savings figure of approximately $2.6 billion between fiscal years 2011 and 2017. As a result of Defense's action, we have removed this recommendation from our report. We have also made changes to the report to reflect these newly-reported numbers. However, in reviewing the additional cost savings information provided by the department, we found that Defense had not fully reported its fiscal years 2012 through 2015 cost savings to OMB, consistent with OMB guidance. As a result, we have added a recommendation for Defense to report all data center consolidation cost savings and avoidances to OMB in accordance with established guidance.

  In written comments, Defense's Acting Principal Deputy CIO stated that the department agreed with the amended report and recommendation.

- In written comments, Energy's CIO stated that the department concurred with the report's recommendation and noted steps being taken by the department to address the discrepancies in its reporting of estimated cost savings and avoidances. For example, the CIO stated that, in order to improve the accuracy and completeness of the data center cost savings and avoidance data, the Energy will clarify its guidance for the integrated data collection data call to better ensure that the department's organizations report on all data center optimization and consolidation activities.
- In comments provided by e-mail on August 25, 2014, an official from HHS's Division for Oversight and Investigations, Assistant Secretary for Legislation, stated that the department concurred with the report's recommendation.
- In comments provided by e-mail on August 11, 2014, an Interior OIG/GAO Audit Liaison stated that the department concurred with the report's findings and recommendations.
- In comments provided by e-mail on August 20, 2014, a Justice audit liaison stated that the department concurred with the report's recommendation.
- In written comments, Labor's Assistant Secretary for Administration and Management and CIO stated that the department concurred with the report's recommendations. The department also provided technical comments, including stating that Labor's data center inventory figures in our draft report were incorrect. Specifically, the department asserted that its total number of data centers was lower than the number cited in our report and that its number of closed data centers was higher. However, the department did not provide supporting documentation for these changes. We have incorporated Labor's other technical comment related to its challenges in achieving cost reductions.
- In written comments, Transportation's Assistant Secretary for Administration stated that the department agreed with the recommendation related to reporting all of its data center consolidation cost savings and avoidances to OMB, but asserted that the department's current reporting of this information satisfied our recommendation. While we acknowledge in our report that Transportation has reported a portion of its cost savings and avoidances to OMB, we identified discrepancies between that information and the cost savings and avoidance information that the

department reported to us. As a result, we determined that Transportation's savings and avoidances were not being fully reported to OMB. Therefore, we continue to believe that our recommendation remains valid.

- In written comments, Treasury's Acting Deputy Assistant Secretary for Information Systems and CIO stated that Treasury had no comments on the report.
- In written comments, VA's Chief of Staff stated that the department concurred with our recommendation to report all data center consolidation cost savings and avoidances to OMB, stating that it plans to begin reporting this information by the end of 2014, but strongly disagreed with our recommendation that OMB include server utilization in the FDCCI metrics. In our report, we acknowledge the reasons that the server utilization metric was not included when OMB issued the data center optimization metrics in May 2014, such as lack of agency data to calculate utilization and lack of utilization monitoring capabilities. However, because low server utilization rates were a driving force in launching FDCCI, we believe that tracking this metric can provide useful information in assessing agencies' progress in optimizing their data centers. As previously mentioned, OMB agreed with our findings and recommendations related to this area. Accordingly, we continue to believe our recommendation remains valid.
- In written comments, EPA's Acting Assistant Administrator and CIO stated that the agency agreed with our findings, conclusions, and recommendation, and noted processes in place to address the recommendation.
- In written comments, GSA's Administrator stated that the agency agreed with the report's findings and recommendation and would take appropriate actions to address the recommendation.
- In written comments, NASA's CIO stated that the agency concurred with one of two of our recommendations and partially concurred with the other. Specifically, NASA agreed with our recommendation related to reporting all of its data center consolidation cost savings and avoidances to OMB, stating that it would issue a directive by October 2014. The agency partially concurred with our recommendation to complete an action plan for addressing challenges in reporting cost savings. Specifically, NASA stated that, while it plans to develop and finalize revisions of existing action plans by December 2014,

execution of those plans remains a challenge due to difficulties in power metering, particularly in older multipurpose buildings, and measuring facility savings. While we acknowledge the challenges described by NASA in our report, we believe that completing an action plan to address these challenges, as we recommended, could serve as a valuable tool in defining a road map toward overcoming these issues. We therefore continue to believe our recommendation remains valid.

- In written comments, OPM's CIO stated that the agency concurred with our recommendation and described planned actions to address our recommendation. For example, the CIO stated that OPM is preparing its data center consolidation plan to include consideration for shared services and cloud technologies and that any related cost savings will be reported once the consolidation plan is implemented.
- In comments provided via e-mail on August 5, 2014, a policy analyst from Education's Office of the Secretary/Executive Secretariat stated that the department had no comments on the report.
- In comments provided via e-mail on August 18, 2014, a program analyst from DHS's Departmental GAO-OIG Liaison Office stated that the department had no technical comments on the report.
- In written comments, HUD's CIO stated that the agency had no comments on the report.
- In comments provided by e-mail on August 8, 2014, a senior management analyst from State's Bureau of the Comptroller and Global Financial Services stated that the agency had no comments on the report.
- In written comments, NSF's CIO stated that the agency had no comments on the report.
- In comments provided via e-mail on August 19, 2014, an executive technical assistant from NRC's Office of the Executive Director for Operations stated that the agency had no comments on the report.
- In comments provided via e-mail on August 12, 2014, the program manager for SBA's Office of Congressional and Legislative Affairs stated that the agency had no comments on the report.
- In written comments, the Deputy Chief of Staff from SSA's Office of the Commissioner stated that the agency had no comments on the report.
- In comments provided via e-mail on August 11, 2014, a systems accountant from USAID's Office of the Chief Financial Officer,

Audit, Performance and Compliance Division, stated that the agency had no comments on the report.

David A. Powner
Director,
Information Technology Management Issues

APPENDIX I: OBJECTIVES, SCOPE, AND METHODOLOGY

Our objectives were to (1) evaluate the extent to which agencies have achieved cost savings to date and identified future savings through their consolidation efforts, (2) identify agencies' notable consolidation successes and challenges in achieving cost savings, and (3) evaluate the extent to which data center optimization metrics have been established.

To evaluate the extent to which agencies have achieved cost savings to date and identified future savings through their consolidation efforts, we obtained and analyzed cost savings and avoidance documentation, relative to requirements of the Office of Management and Budget's (OMB) March 2013 memorandum,[1] from the 24 departments and agencies (agencies) in our review.[2] This documentation included, but was not limited to, agencies' quarterly reports of cost savings and avoidances submitted to OMB, total cost of ownership[3] models, contract and budget documentation, and internal agency status reports. To determine cost savings achieved to date, we totaled agency reported savings and avoidances from fiscal years 2011 through 2013, and to identify future planned savings we totaled agency projected savings and avoidances from fiscal years 2014 through 2017.[4] We also compared agencies' cost savings and avoidance information to key requirements for identifying and reporting data center consolidation cost savings and avoidances, as outlined in OMB's March 2013 memorandum.

To assess the reliability of agencies' cost savings and avoidance data, we reviewed related documentation provided by agency data center program managers and other cognizant officials, such as agency total cost of ownership models, agency-developed spreadsheets, agencies' quarterly data submissions to OMB, among other sources. We also compared the cost savings and avoidances reported to us by agencies with cost savings identified in OMB's quarterly reports to Congress on the status of information technology reform efforts.[5] In addition, we reviewed agency documentation for missing data or other errors (e.g., incorrect calculations). Finally, we interviewed agency officials to obtain additional supporting information regarding how their cost savings and avoidance figures were determined, the processes and methods to recalculate the figures, and the steps that the agency took to ensure the reliability of their figures and validate their figures. We also discussed with agency officials any discrepancies or potential errors identified during our review of their supporting documentation to determine the cause or request additional information. We determined that the data were sufficiently reliable to report on agencies' cost savings achieved to date and identified future savings. However, as part of our reliability assessment, we identified issues with the reliability of OMB's quarterly reports to Congress, including that agencies' data center consolidation cost savings were not being fully reflected in OMB's report. We have highlighted this issue in our report.

Lastly, we reviewed agencies' data center facility reductions as reported on http://data.gov and compared the information to agencies' cost savings and avoidances achieved to date, taking into consideration the challenges in achieving savings identified by agencies. To assess the reliability of agencies' data center reductions, we reviewed prior reporting of data center closures to check for anomalies in the data, such as fewer closures for agencies in more recent data sets than previously reported. We also checked for missing data, outliers, and other obvious errors, such as missing closure status information. Finally, we interviewed OMB staff from the Office of E-Government and Information Technology regarding actions taken to verify the data. We determined that the data were sufficiently reliable to report on agencies' consolidation progress.

To identify notable consolidation successes and challenges in achieving cost savings, we reviewed agencies' cost savings documentation, including quarterly reports on cost savings and avoidances submitted to OMB, total cost of ownership models, contract and budget documentation, internal agency status reports, and other documentation, and interviewed agency officials. To determine the types of successes experienced, we identified areas reported in agencies' documentation with directly attributable cost savings or avoidances. We also interviewed agency officials to identify additional successes in achieving cost savings, including areas where the agency may not have been able to quantify the savings. To determine challenges in achieving cost savings, we interviewed agency officials to obtain information regarding challenges faced, as well as to discuss any steps taken, or planned, to address the challenges identified. We then determined which successes and challenges were encountered most often. In some cases, agencies' cost savings and avoidance data were used to highlight the impact of a particular success. As a result of the reliability assessment performed for our first objective, we determined these data to be sufficiently reliable for reporting on agencies' cost savings and avoidances achieved to date and planned.

To evaluate the extent to which data center optimization metrics have been established, we analyzed OMB's March 2013 memorandum[6] to determine OMB's requirements for such metrics, including the responsibilities for completing the metrics and the key areas or categories that were to be addressed by the metrics. We then compared OMB's requirements for the metrics to the final metrics, as documented in a May 2014 OMB memorandum.[7] We also reviewed previous data center consolidation-related OMB memorandums[8] and consolidation plan guidance to identify metrics that had previously been identified by OMB as indicators of data center optimization success and determined the extent to which the metrics addressed these areas. Finally, we interviewed relevant OMB, General Services Administration, and Data Center Consolidation Task Force officials to discuss the process by which the metrics were established and to determine the extent that related targets, or goals, for the metrics had been established.

We conducted this performance audit from October 2013 to September 2014 in accordance with generally accepted government auditing standards. Those standards require that we plan and perform the audit to obtain sufficient, appropriate evidence to provide a reasonable basis for our findings and conclusions based on our audit objectives. We believe that the evidence obtained provides a reasonable basis for our findings and conclusions based on our audit objectives.

End Notes

[1] GAO, Data Center Consolidation: Strengthened Oversight Needed to Achieve Cost Savings Goal, GAO-13-378 (Washington, D.C.: Apr. 23, 2013); Data Center Consolidation: Agencies Making Progress on Efforts, but Inventories and Plans Need to Be Completed, GAO-12-742 (Washington, D.C.: July 19, 2012); and Data Center Consolidation: Agencies Need to Complete Inventories and Plans to Achieve Expected Savings, GAO-11-565 (Washington, D.C.: July 19, 2011).

[2] GAO, Information Technology: Reform Initiatives Can Help Improve Efficiency and Effectiveness, GAO-14-671T (Washington, D.C.: June 10, 2014); Information Technology: Implementing Best Practices and Reform Initiatives Can Help Improve the Management of Investments, GAO-14-596T (Washington, D.C.: May 8, 2014); Information Technology: OMB and Agencies Need to More Effectively Implement Major Initiatives to Save Billions of Dollars, GAO-13-796T (Washington, D.C.: July 25, 2013); Information Technology: OMB and Agencies Need to Focus Continued Attention on Eliminating Duplicative

Investments, GAO-13-685T (Washington, D.C.: June 11, 2013); and Data Center Consolidation: Strengthened Oversight Needed to Achieve Billions of Dollars in Savings, GAO-13-627T (Washington, D.C.: May 14, 2013).

[3] The 24 major departments and agencies that participate in FDCCI are the Departments of Agriculture, Commerce, Defense, Education, Energy, Health and Human Services, Homeland Security, Housing and Urban Development, the Interior, Justice, Labor, State, Transportation, the Treasury, and Veterans Affairs; the Environmental Protection Agency, General Services Administration, National Aeronautics and Space Administration, National Science Foundation, Nuclear Regulatory Commission, Office of Personnel Management, Small Business Administration, Social Security Administration, and U.S. Agency for International Development.

[4] OMB, Fiscal Year 2013 PortfolioStat Guidance: Strengthening Federal IT Portfolio Management, Memorandum M-13-09 (Washington, D.C.: Mar. 27, 2013).

[5] OMB, Memorandum M-13-09.

[6] OMB, Inventory of Federal Data Center Activity, Budget Data Request No. 09-41 (Washington, D.C.: Aug. 10, 2009).

[7] "Green IT" refers to environmentally sound computing practices that can include a variety of efforts, such as using energy-efficient data centers, purchasing computers that meet certain environmental standards, and recycling obsolete electronics.

[8] Pub. L. No. 111-352, 124 Stat. 3866 (Jan. 4, 2011). GPRAMA significantly enhanced the Government Performance and Results Act of 1993, Pub. L. No. 103-62, 107 Stat. 285 (Aug. 3, 1993).

[9] For more information on the classifications used to define availability requirements, see Uptime Institute, Industry Standard Tier Classifications Define Site Infrastructure Performance (Santa Fe, N.Mex.: 2005).

[10] OMB, Implementation Guidance for the Federal Data Center Consolidation Initiative (Washington, D.C.: Mar. 19, 2012).

[11] GAO-13-796T.

[12] According to OMB, as of July 2014, the total number of data centers collectively reported by agencies was 9,540, of which 275 were reported as core data centers and 9,265 were reported as non-core centers. OMB's tally of data centers differs from the number of data centers we found because, as we have previously reported, the number of data centers changes regularly as agencies update their inventories.

[13] According to OMB, commodity IT includes services such as IT infrastructure (data centers, networks, desktop computers and mobile devices); enterprise IT systems (e-mail, collaboration tools, identity and access management, security, and web infrastructure); and business systems (finance, human resources, and other administrative functions).

[14] OMB, Implementing PortfolioStat, Memorandum M-12-10 (Washington D.C.: Mar. 30, 2012).

[15] OMB, Memorandum M-13-09.

[16] OMB, Management of Federal Information Resources, Circular A-130 (Washington, D.C.: Nov. 30, 2000). According to OMB Circular A-130, an agency's information resources management strategic plan should describe how information resources management activities help accomplish agency missions, and ensure that information resource management decisions are integrated with organizational planning, budget, procurement, financial management, human resources management, and program decisions.

[17] OMB, Increasing Shared Approaches to Information Technology Services (Washington, D.C.: May 2, 2012). The enterprise road map is to include a business and technology architecture,

an IT asset inventory, a commodity IT consolidation plan, a line of business service plan, and an IT shared service plan.

[18] According to OMB, the integrated data collection channel is to be used by agencies to report structured information, such as progress in meeting IT strategic goals, objectives, and metrics, as well as cost savings and avoidances resulting from IT management actions.

[19] OMB, Fiscal Year 2014 PortfolioStat, Memorandum M-14-08 (Washington, D.C.: May 7, 2014).

[20] GAO, Opportunities to Reduce Potential Duplication in Government Programs, Save Tax Dollars, and Enhance Revenue, GAO-11-318SP (Washington, D.C.: Mar. 1, 2011).

[21] GAO-11-565.

[22] GAO-12-742.

[23] OMB refers to total cost of ownership as all associated data center-related activities and costs without regard to ownership, project association, or funding line.

[24] GAO-13-378.

[25] GAO-14-671T, GAO-14-596T, GAO-13-796T, GAO-13-685T, and GAO-13-627T.

[26] As previously mentioned, as of May 2014, agencies had collectively reported a total of 9,658 data centers—an increase of 2,822 compared to what agencies had reported as of July 2013.

[27] OMB budget guidance defines cost savings as a reduction in actual expenditures below the projected level of costs to achieve a specific objective and defines cost avoidances as results from an action taken in the immediate time frame that will decrease costs in the future.

[28] OMB, Memorandum M-13-09. According to OMB's guidance, the integrated data collection is to be used by agencies to report structured information, such as progress in meeting IT strategic goals, objectives, and metrics, as well as cost savings and avoidances resulting from IT management actions, including data center consolidation.

[29] GAO-13-378.

[30] OMB, Memorandum M-13-09.

[31] OMB, Memorandum M-14-08.

[32] GAO, Standards for Internal Control in the Federal Government, GAO-14-704G (Washington, D.C.: Sept. 10, 2014).

[33] OMB, Memorandum M-14-08.

[34] GAO, Information Technology: Additional OMB and Agency Actions Are Needed to Achieve Portfolio Savings, GAO-14-65 (Washington, D.C.: Nov. 6, 2013).

[35] We have ongoing work looking at the status of the required fiscal year 2013 PortfolioStat actions, including agencies holding PortfolioStat sessions.

[36] Three agencies—the Department of Housing and Urban Development, the Small Business Administration, and the U.S. Agency for International Development—did not have actual or estimated savings or avoidances between fiscal years 2012 and 2015.

[37] OMB, Quarterly Report to Congress: Information Technology Oversight and Reform (Washington, D.C.: May 6, 2014).

[38] Agencies did not always have reportable cost savings or avoidances in areas noted as successes due, in part, to challenges in quantifying their savings and avoidances (as discussed throughout this report).

[39] GAO-12-742.

[40] See Pub. L. No. 112-81, § 2867, 125 Stat. 1298, 1704 (2011).

[41] GAO-11-565 and GAO-12-742.

[42] GAO-11-565.

[43] GAO, Aviation Weather: Agencies Need to Improve Performance Measurement and Fully Address Key Challenges, GAO-10-843 (Washington, D.C.: Sept. 9, 2011); GAO, NextGen

Air Transportation System: FAA's Metrics Can Be Used to Report on Status of Individual Programs, but Not of Overall NextGen Implementation or Outcomes, GAO-10-629 (Washington, D.C.: July 27, 2010); OMB, Guide to the Program Assessment Rating Tool (Washington, D.C.: January 2008); Department of the Navy, Office of the Chief Information Officer, Guide for Developing and Using IT Performance Measurements (Washington, D.C.: October 2001); and GSA, Performance-Based Management: Eight Steps To Develop and Use Information Technology Performance Measures Effectively (Washington, D.C.: 1996).

[44] OMB, Memorandum M-13-09.

[45] OMB, Memorandum M-14-08.

[46] OMB, Inventory of Federal Data Center Activity, Budget Data Request No. 09-41 (Washington, D.C.: Aug. 10, 2009).

[47] OMB, Memorandum M-13-09.

End Notes for Appendix I

[1] OMB, Fiscal Year 2013 PortfolioStat Guidance: Strengthening Federal IT Portfolio Management, Memorandum M-13-09 (Washington, D.C.: Mar. 27, 2013).

[2] The 24 major departments and agencies that participate in the Federal Data Center Consolidation Initiative are the Departments of Agriculture, Commerce, Defense, Education, Energy, Health and Human Services, Homeland Security, Housing and Urban Development, the Interior, Justice, Labor, State, Transportation, the Treasury, and Veterans Affairs; the Environmental Protection Agency, General Services Administration, National Aeronautics and Space Administration, National Science Foundation, Nuclear Regulatory Commission, Office of Personnel Management, Small Business Administration, Social Security Administration, and U.S. Agency for International Development.

[3] OMB refers to total cost of ownership as all associated data center-related activities and costs without regard to ownership, project association, or funding line.

[4] Three agencies—the Department of Housing and Urban Development, the Small Business Administration, and the U.S. Agency for International Development—reported no cost savings to date or planned future savings.

[5] OMB, Quarterly Report to Congress: Information Technology Oversight and Reform (Washington, D.C.: May 6, 2014) and Quarterly Report to Congress: Integrated, Efficient, and Effective Uses of Information Technology (Washington, D.C.: Feb. 18, 2014).

[6] OMB, Memorandum M-13-09.

[7] OMB, Fiscal Year 2014 PortfolioStat, Memorandum M-14-08 (Washington, D.C.: May 7, 2014).

[8] See, for example, OMB, Update on the Federal Data Center Consolidation Initiative (Washington, D.C.: Oct. 1, 2010); Federal Data Center Consolidation Initiative (Washington, D.C.: Feb. 26, 2010); and Inventory of Federal Data Center Activity, Budget Data Request No. 09-41 (Washington, D.C.: Aug. 10, 2009).

In: Federal Data Center Consolidation
Editor: Patricia L. Winslow
ISBN: 978-1-63463-896-8

Chapter 2

Department of Defense Implementation of the Federal Data Center Consolidation Initiative: Implications for Federal Information Technology Reform Management*

Patricia Moloney Figliola, Anthony Andrews and Eric A. Fischer

Summary

The Department of Defense (DOD) is the single largest energy consumer in the nation. As the largest owner of federal data centers, with 772, the DOD has more than twice as many centers as any other agency. By consolidating some of its data centers, DOD could have a significant positive impact on energy savings for the federal government. DOD has instituted a number of policy directives, as have all federal agencies, that influence energy use in its data centers.

* This is an edited, reformatted and augmented version of a Congressional Research Service publication R42604, prepared for Members and Committees of Congress, dated April 23, 2013.

Data centers are facilities—buildings or parts of buildings—used to store, manage, and disseminate electronic information for a computer network. They house servers, which are computers used to perform network-management functions such as data storage and processing, and communications equipment and devices to connect the servers with the network. Data centers usually draw their power from the electric grid, but they may also contain specialized power conversion and backup equipment to maintain reliable power. Power consumption varies greatly among data centers but is typically many times higher than for other kinds of buildings.

Within the context of the FDCCI, DOD's efforts are intended to address concerns about rising energy demands and costs of data centers, associated increases in carbon emissions, expanding real-estate footprints of data centers, and rising real-estate costs. According to DOD, the Department plans to reduce the number of its data centers by about 30% by 2013, and the number of servers by 25%. DOD intends to use savings generated from consolidation to pay the consolidation costs. DOD also plans to use cloud computing as part of its savings effort.

As with any endeavor being implemented across so many departments and agencies, proper management of the initiative will be crucial to its success and, in turn, to achieving the projected savings. Unlike many programs that are overseen by a single committee, implementation of the FDCCI may require oversight by any committee with legislative jurisdiction over a department or agency. Understanding the management challenges and policy considerations involved with data center consolidation (e.g., balancing up-front costs with ongoing savings, maintaining data security, and maximizing energy savings through facilities design) as well as being aware of the issues specific to implementing the FDCCI are important steps to achieving effective Congressional oversight of the FDCCI. In conducting oversight, Congress may wish to

- conduct hearings to monitor the activities of OMB as it manages the FDCCI or the progress of individual departments and agencies as they implement the FDCCI;
- review FDCCI plans and status reports created internally by the individual department or agency, or externally by the Government Accountability Office (GAO) or the committee of jurisdiction.

Finally, Congress may wish to examine the current "reach" of the FDCCI and consider whether expanding the initiative to include other agencies, as GAO has recommended, is appropriate.

INTRODUCTION

The Department of Defense (DOD) is the single largest energy consumer in the nation, accounting for approximately 63% of the energy consumed by federal buildings/facilities at an annual cost of $3.4 billion (FY2007). A significant component of that energy use entails data storage. As of this date, DOD has twice as many data centers as any other federal agency. By consolidating some of those data centers, DOD could have a significant positive impact on energy savings for the federal government.

Consolidating data centers run by the DOD has been an ongoing effort that began in 1989 with an internal study, *Consolidate ADP Operations and Design Centers in DOD*, and continues today through the Federal Data Center Consolidation Initiative (FDCCI).[1] The FDCCI is intended to reverse the growth in potentially redundant IT infrastructure throughout the federal agencies and mitigate the impact such redundancy has on federal energy consumption.[2]

This report provides the context and background of the FDCCI, using DOD data center consolidation as an example of the government's work in this area. The report provides an overview of data center characteristics, specifically the technology used, power consumption issues, and how data centers are classified. It summarizes how and why the federal government increased its investment in data centers and then later determined that consolidation was a better path forward based on the state of computing and communications technology. The report goes on to describe the historical legislation underlying the current initiative, and concludes with a discussion of possible issues for Congressional oversight or consideration.

GENERAL DATA CENTER CHARACTERISTICS

Data centers are facilities—buildings or parts of buildings—used to store, manage, and disseminate electronic information for a computer network. They house servers, which are computers used to perform network-management functions such as data storage and processing, and communications equipment and devices to connect the servers with the network. These facilities may range in size from small rooms called server closets, or even parts of rooms, within a conventional building, to large dedicated buildings called enterprise-class data centers. Larger centers may be purpose-built or retrofitted.

Data centers usually draw their power from the electric grid, but they may also contain specialized power conversion and backup equipment to maintain reliable power, as well as environmental control equipment to maintain the proper temperature and humidity for the information technology (IT) equipment.

Users generally access data-center resources via workstations, laptop computers, or other devices running software, such as an Internet browser, that interacts with server software. Many software applications require not just data processing, which drives computing demand, but also large amounts of data storage, which drives the demand for storage equipment in data centers.

Advances in computing technology and related changes in power consumption are the two factors that have driven data center capabilities and trends.

Technology

Over the past several decades, computer processing speeds have increased exponentially while the central processing units (CPU) at the heart of computers have reduced in size. Advanced processing chips have allowed manufacturers to pack more processing into smaller and smaller hardware, allowing a higher ratio of computing power to floor space. This trend, commonly referred to as "increased server rack density," has also led to higher power densities in many data centers. Such increased densities result in increased production of heat, which must be removed to maintain servers within their normal operating ranges. Consequently, cooling the CPU consumes additional power, often more than the CPU consumes itself.

Data center rooms are filled with rows of IT equipment racks that contain servers, storage devices, and network equipment. Data centers include power delivery systems that provide backup power, regulate voltage, and make necessary power conversions. Before reaching the IT equipment rack, electricity is first supplied to an uninterruptible power supply (UPS) unit. The UPS acts as a battery backup to prevent the IT equipment from experiencing power disruptions, which could cause serious business disruption or data loss. In the UPS, the electricity is converted from AC to DC to charge the batteries. Power from the batteries is then reconverted from DC to AC before leaving the UPS. Power leaving the UPS enters a power distribution unit, which sends power directly to the IT equipment in the racks. Electricity consumed in this power delivery chain accounts for a substantial portion of overall building load.

Power Consumption

Power consumption varies greatly among data centers but is typically many times higher than for other kinds of buildings. According to the Federal Energy Management Program (FEMP), a data center can consume as much as 100 times the energy of a typical office building.

Virtually all of the power consumed by a data center results in thermal emissions: Ultimately, a watt of electric power consumed is a watt of heat generated. Data centers use energy to supply three key components: IT equipment, cooling, and power delivery. A significant amount of energy is required just to remove heat (see *Figure 1*). A breakdown of a data center's energy use may show that cooling alone may make up half of its electrical demand, while operating the servers and data storage devices (critical loads) may take up a third or more. Lighting and charging battery-backup UPS make up the balance.

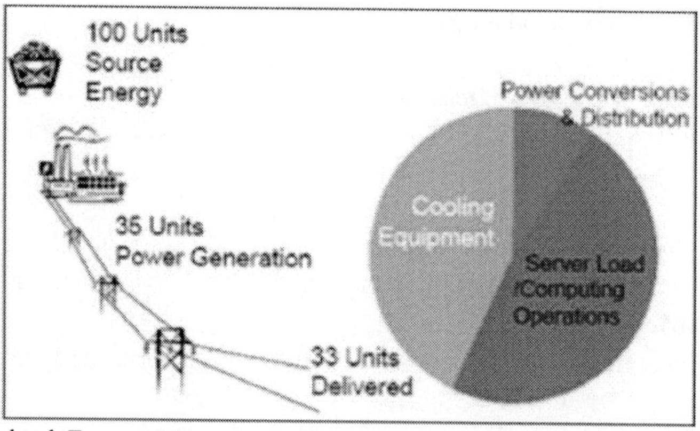

Source: Federal Energy Management Program, "Data Center Energy Consumption Trends," May 30, 2009.

Notes: The figure shows how a data center typically uses energy. Inefficiencies in the generation and transmission of electric power result in only about one-third of the source energy (e.g., from coal or natural gas) being delivered as electricity to the data center. Less than half of that electricity is typically used for computing operations.

Figure 1. A Typical Data Center Energy Use Pattern.

Energy-efficient servers are available. The Environmental Protection Agency (EPA) and the Department of Energy (DOE) have developed a specification that servers must meet to receive the Energy Star label. The Federal Acquisition Regulations require agencies to purchase Energy Star products or products designated as energy-efficient under FEMP. In addition, the Institute of Electrical and Electronic Engineers (IEEE), an accredited standards development organization, has begun the process of developing standards for assigning the green "EPEAT"[3] label to qualifying servers. Federal agencies are required to procure EPEAT-registered products for 95% of acquisitions of products for which the label is available.

As server power becomes more concentrated and servers become more energy-efficient, one impact is that, in many cases, power and cooling capacity will be the primary constraints to the expansion of computational capacity within a data center. Server hardware would no longer be the primary cost component of a data center. This represents a significant shift in data center economics that threatens to overwhelm the advances in chip efficiency that have driven the growth of digital information during the past 30 years.

As a result, data center managers must either invest in upgrading the power and cooling infrastructure of existing data centers, or they must build new facilities. Either choice requires significant capital investment and must also include operational changes.

Power Rating vs. Power Demand

Data center managers must also consider hardware's power rating and power demand:

- Power rating is the amount of electrical power that a piece of electronic equipment is designed to draw if it is running at full capacity.
- Power demand is the amount of power the server actually uses.

Power demand may, in fact, be much lower than the power rating. A server's power consumption will vary depending on the type of server, its power management characteristics, and its use of other IT resources. Estimating a data center's power demand by examining each component's specification sheet yields only the potential maximum power consumption.

In fact, data centers are typically planned to exceed the maximum future estimated power requirements for the expected load. As a result, they are typically oversized, with overall power ratings that exceed true demand requirements—the maximum actual power load drawn by operating servers and cooling equipment—by more than 100% of the required capacity. Such oversizing is often done with the goal of maximizing reliability in the face of expected growth in use.

Throughout the 1990s, servers operated at nearly constant power demands, as the computational load placed on processors and memory caused a negligible variation in overall power consumption. Most servers operate at low computational loads most of the time, and those with power management capability will draw less than their potential power draw. However, the power draw can vary dynamically, such as a power variation of more than 100% between a light-load and a heavy-load draw.

Until recently, data center design and operation has focused on reliability and capacity, with energy efficiency at best a secondary consideration. Some studies indicate that data centers may be using more energy than they need to, even taking reliability needs into account. For example, a 2012 research study conducted by IBM found that one in five data centers was operating at optimum efficiency.[4]

One way to improve data-center energy efficiency is to require users to pay for the energy they actually use. That requires metering. However, for data centers with a wide range of servers, allocating energy costs to users becomes impractical because much of the energy use comes from power equipment, cooling equipment, network devices and other loads not directly associated with a particular user. Furthermore, the cost of metering a particular server and the software required can be extreme. Alternatively, the data center manager can classify servers into a short list of standard types, each with its own energy profile. This would permit allocating total data-center energy across a number of server classes, in order to assign use to individual IT users. Such rationing might be an alternative or a supplement to metering for individual users.

Power Usage Effectiveness (PUE), developed by Green Grid (a global IT consortium) is a metric for data-center energy efficiency that is becoming widely used. PUE is measured by dividing the total electrical power used by a data center by the power used by the IT equipment. Thus, if a data center had a PUE of 2.0, half the power would be consumed by the IT equipment and the other half by other facility components such as cooling, battery back-ups, and so forth. According to EPA, most data centers exhibit a PUE of 1.25 to 3.0.

THE DATA CENTER TREND ARC: FROM GROWTH TO CONSOLIDATION

Worldwide energy use by data centers doubled from 2000 to 2006.[5] During this time, federal agencies built up their data centers independently, leading to a day-to-day surplus of computing power. Because of the energy demands created by this independent growth, the federal government began considering ways to consolidate data centers and find a more cost-effective means of providing sufficient computing power to its agencies while decreasing energy use.

Growth

According to some reports, worldwide energy use by data centers doubled from 2000 to 2006 and a number of factors continue to drive such growth. Among them are electronic financial transactions such as online banking and electronic trading, Internet communication and entertainment, electronic medical records for healthcare, global commerce and services, satellite navigation, and electronic shipment tracking in transportation. Voice-over-Internet protocol[6] communication has also been growing. Increased Internet use is a major factor in the growth in data processing and storage and requires that business and government enterprises host electronic applications in highly reliable data centers with sufficient server capacity to meet peak and growing loads.

Factors contributing to increased use by government include publishing government information and regulations; enhancing disaster recovery, emergency, health and safety services; migrating toward increased "e-government" services (e.g., e-filing of taxes); and access to remote highspeed computing. Government agencies must increase public website hosting to provide online reports and information, and other digital services (e.g., e-filing of taxes, online tracking of items sent through the U.S. Postal Service). In addition, requirements related to homeland security (from e-passports to cybersecurity) and scientific computing in government research institutions add additional IT burdens. State and local governments are also subject to many of the same demands.

In addition to their everyday business-related computer applications, companies are increasingly subject to regulations that require them to collect and store digital records of their business transactions. The most well known regulation is the Sarbanes-Oxley Act, which requires longterm storage of financial records, including electronic records such as email. According to some projections, the number of records that some industries must retain grew at an estimated compound annual growth rate (CAGR) of 50% or greater in the last decade. Business disaster recovery needs are also strong motivators for increasing storage (e.g., duplicate data sets) and establishing redundant data-center equipment and facilities.

Consolidation

Data center consolidation, both in the private and public sectors, has been an increasing trend for several years (*Figure 2*). The general pattern is consolidation of many smaller data centers into one data center or a few larger ones. Several factors, mostly related to costs, have been cited as contributing to this trend. Among them are the following:

- more efficient use of servers, storage, and staff, including reductions in energy consumed by idle servers;
- reductions in redundancy of hardware, software, and operations requirements, including HVAC;
- increased flexibility in use of servers;
- freed up floor space for other purposes;
- increased reliability of service; and
- improved security.

Consolidation from a cost-saving perspective may be particularly attractive during times of economic downturn, as it can apparently produce substantial cost savings. For example, for many data centers, under 10% of the servers' capacity is typically used, even though data centers can account for about one-quarter of total IT costs for large enterprises. Annual costs for those facilities are increasing at 10% per year, more than thrice the growth rate of other IT spending.

Given such costs, growth, and inefficiencies, it may seem surprising that more effort has not been made to address them. At least two factors have been cited to explain that pattern.

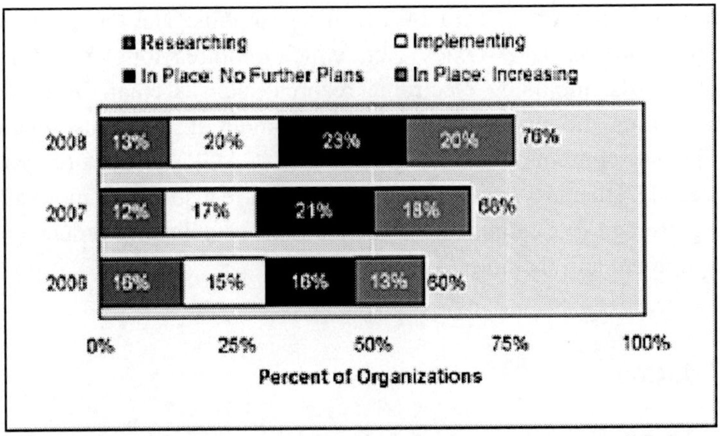

Source: Computer Economics, Inc., "Data Center Consolidation Shows Overwhelmingly Positive ROI," August 2008, http://www.computereconomics.com/article.cfm?id=1386.

Notes: The data are from a survey of more than 200 organizations of various sizes.

Figure 2. Data Center Consolidation Trends, 2006 to 2008. Percentages of Surveyed Organizations Citing Specific Actions.

First, the traditional focus of data-center management has primarily been on service and reliability in response to rising demand. This can reduce the priority of efforts to improve energy efficiency and cost savings. Second, organizational fragmentation in the management of data centers—for example, by separating financial from operational responsibilities—and "siloing" of decisions have been cited as significant barriers. As a result, decisions that lead to increased demand may be made with little or no regard to their impacts on data-center energy use and costs.

The goals of the FDCCI largely reflect those factors. (The FDCCI is discussed in detail in the section below, "The Federal Data Center Consolidation Initiative.")

BUILDING TOWARDS THE CURRENT CONSOLIDATION INITIATIVE

Three documents form the basis of the current consolidation initiative by the federal government.

National Performance Review and OMB Bulletin 96-02, Consolidation of Agency Data Centers

In 1993, the Vice President's National Performance Review recommended that the federal government take advantage of evolving technology to consolidate information-processing services to decrease costs. The Office of Management and Budget (OMB) followed up with Bulletin 96-02—*Consolidation of Agency Data Centers*—which called on federal agencies to consolidate and modernize their data centers, collocate small and mid-tier computer platforms, and outsource small-scale information processing either to other agencies or commercial enterprises.

The Review and OMB bulletin estimated that 30%-50% savings could be obtained in an operational costs report on information infrastructure and "industry experience." While the performance review did include a proposal for an executive order on energy efficiency and water conservation at federal facilities, it made no specific link between energy efficiency and IT. Consolidation of data centers (in the interest of energy-efficiency improvement) appears to be a recent rationale, although energy savings mandates across federal agencies date back several decades.

EPA Report to Congress on Server and Data Center Energy Efficiency

In December 2006, Congress mandated that the EPA study the use of energy efficient computer servers. P.L. 109-431[7] required that the EPA, through the Energy Star program, study and report on the rapid growth and energy consumption of computer data centers by the federal government and private enterprise. The EPA responded with its "Report to Congress on Server and Data Center Energy Efficiency" in August 2007 ("*EPA Report*").[8] This report illustrated the nexus between data center IT and energy consumption and demonstrated the government's commitment to federal IT reform to support energy conservation and savings.

In the *EPA Report*, published in August 2007, the agency estimated that U.S. data servers had accounted for roughly 1.5% of total U.S. electric consumption in 2006, for approximately 61 billion kWh at a cost of about $4.5 billion. That same year, federal servers and data centers reportedly accounted for approximately 6 billion kWh at a cost of about $450 million—about 10%

of that national total use. The *EPA Report* also presented estimates that data-center electricity use in 2006 was more than double than in 2000, and noted that the power and cooling infrastructure supporting that server equipment accounted for 50% of the total consumption.

Projections of Future Data Center Energy Use

The EPA Report developed two five-year projections for data-center energy trends:

- The *current efficiency trends* scenario projected future energy use of U.S. servers and data centers based on observed efficiency trends for IT equipment and site infrastructure systems.
- The *historical trends* scenario did not reflect energy efficiency trends but simply extrapolated observed 2000-2006 energy-use trends into the future. It assumed no future energy-efficiency improvements, and therefore indicated the energy savings already under way.

Under *current efficiency trends,* the report stated that national energy consumption by servers and data centers could nearly double in another five years (i.e., by 2011) to more than 100 billion kWh, representing a $7.4 billion annual electricity cost. The server's and data center's estimated 7-GW peak load on the power grid equaled the output of "about 15 baseload power plants."

The report went on to say that if current trends were to continue, this demand would rise to 12 GW by 2011, "which would require an additional 10 power plants." Those forecasts indicated that unless energy efficiency improved beyond then-current trends, the federal government's electricity cost for servers and data centers could be nearly $740 million annually by 2011, with a peak load of approximately 1.2 GW.

Energy Efficiency

The EPA Report stated that there is significant potential for energy-efficiency improvements in data centers. Although some improvements in energy efficiency were expected if current trends continued, many technologies, either commercially available or soon available, could further improve the energy efficiency of microprocessors, servers, storage devices, network equipment, and infrastructure systems. Other opportunities could accelerate adoption of energy-efficient technologies beyond current trends:

- The *improved operation* scenario included energy-efficiency improvements beyond current trends that are essentially operational in nature and require little or no capital investment. This scenario offered potential electricity savings of more than 20% relative to then-current trends, representing low-cost energy-efficiency opportunities.
- The *best practice* scenario represented the efficiency gains that more widespread adoption of the practices and technologies could obtain using the most energy-efficient facilities in operation. This scenario could reduce electricity use by up to The *state-of-the-art* scenario identified the maximum energy-efficiency savings that available technologies could achieve. This scenario could reduce electricity use by up to 55% compared to then-current efficiency trends, representing the maximum technical potential.

According to the report, those scenarios showed an annual savings potential of about 23 billion-74 billion kWh in 2011 compared to the *current efficiency trends* scenario, reducing the peak load from data centers by the equivalent of up to 15 new power plants and reducing annual electricity costs by $1.6 bilion-$5.1 billion. Based on the assumption that the federal sector accounts for about 10% of electricity use and electricity costs attributable to servers and data centers, the annual savings in federal electricity costs in 2011 could range from $160 million (*improved operation*) to $510 million (*state-of-the-art*). Those gains could be achieved without compromising performance.

Executive Order 13514, Federal Leadership in Environmental, Energy, and Economic Performance

On October 5, 2009, President Obama signed Executive Order 13514, *Federal Leadership in Environmental, Energy, and Economic Performance.*[9] This order directs federal agencies to establish an integrated strategy towards sustainability and makes reductions in greenhouse gas emissions a priority. It also requires federal agencies to increase energy efficiency and "implement best management practices for energy-efficient management of servers and Federal data centers." The order also increases the energy efficiency levels required of new building designs, and sets a target of zero net-energy consumption for new buildings by 2030. It encourages cost-effective, innovative strategies to minimize water and energy consumption—for example, reflective or vegetated roofs. Rehabilitation of federally owned, historic buildings should employ "best practices" and technologies to promote long-term viability. The order also gives priority to the developing site selection procedures to site federal buildings in sustainable locations.

THE FEDERAL DATA CENTER CONSOLIDATION INITIATIVE

Building on the *EPA Report* and in tandem with Executive Order 13514, as well as in light of the benefits of data center consolidation reported by private sector, in February 2010, the U.S. Chief Information Officer (CIO) announced the FDCCI.[10] The four high-level goals of the initiative are to:[11]

1. promote the use of "Green IT"[12] by reducing the overall energy and real estate footprint of government data centers;[13]
2. reduce the cost of data center hardware, software, and operations;
3. increase the overall IT security posture of the government; and
4. shift IT investments to more efficient computing platforms and technologies.

The initiative is intended to reverse the growth in potentially redundant IT infrastructure throughout the federal agencies and its significant impact on federal energy consumption.[14]

OMB was charged with executing and managing the initiative and it, in turn, designated two CIOs for each of the 24 participating departments and agencies.[15] OMB required that the agencies submit data center inventories and consolidation plans by the end of August 2010, and provided guidance on key elements to include in the inventories and plans—such as hardware and software assets, goals, schedules, and cost-benefit calculations.

Since the FDCCI was announced, OMB expanded the definition of a data center from facilities over 500 square feet to one that includes data centers of all sizes. This change resulted in an expanded data center baseline of 3,133 centers, an increase from the 2,094 centers originally reported by agencies. In December 2011, the U.S. CIO announced a revised goal of closing over 1,200 of the 3,133 data centers, which was included in the Analytical Perspectives for the President's budget for FY2013.[16] That revision is expected to save $3 billion by 2015.

25-Point Implementation Plan to Reform Federal IT Management

In December 2010, the U.S. CIO released, "A 25-Point Implementation Plan to Reform Federal IT Management."[17] Data center consolidation is the first of the 25 goals outlined: agencies must complete detailed implementation plans for consolidating at least 800 of its 2,100 data centers by 2015—a reduction of almost 40%. By July 2011, 81 data centers had been closed and 373 more were slated for closure by the end of 2012.[18]

One related goal is to create a government-wide marketplace for data center availability, aimed at improving use of existing facilities across agencies. Another related goal is shift to a "cloud first" policy[19] across federal agencies. Cloud computing, a rapidly growing means of using computer resources, could reportedly accelerate the consolidation effort, amplify its benefits by reducing duplication of effort and improving efficiency of use, and simplify IT management.

Status of the FDCCI

At the request of Congress, in July 2011, the Government Accountability Office (GAO) published its findings regarding the status of the FDCCI.[20] In its investigation, it found that only one agency (the National Science Foundation) had submitted a complete inventory and no agency had submitted complete plans. However, agency plans still indicated savings of about $700 million through 2015.

In May 2012, GAO provided Congress with a status report on the 25-Point Plan[21] and its work related to implementing the GPRA Modernization Act,[22] which included an update of FDCCI implementation. In those reports, GAO stated that it was continually assessing the updated inventories and plans that departments and agencies had begun posting online in October 2011. As of April 2012, not all agency inventories and plans had been updated to include all required information, such as consolidation milestones, performance metrics, and savings projections.

DEPARTMENT OF DEFENSE DATA CENTER CONSOLIDATION

DOD accounts for approximately 63% of the energy consumed by federal buildings and other facilities. The department's activities occupy more than 316,000 buildings and an additional 182,000 structures on 536 military installations worldwide. DOD's annual spending on facility energy use was more than $3.4 billion in FY2007. This makes DOD the single largest energy consumer in the nation, even though the agency consumption comprises only 1% of the national total for site-consumed energy.

As the largest owner of federal data centers, with 772 (*Figure 3*), DOD and its military and other constituent services face a complex challenge in implementing the FDCCI. To its benefit in adhering to the schedule for the current initiative, however, DOD has engaged in consolidation efforts over the past few years. In addition, the Secretary of Defense has identified consolidation of IT infrastructure as one of the department's efficiency initiatives announced in August 2010.

DOD has instituted a number of policy directives, as have all federal agencies, that have and will continue to influence energy use in DOD data centers, although most are not targeted specifically to data centers. The FDCCI could lead to a reduction in data-center energy use, at least in the short term. However, in the face of what is likely to be continuously increasing demand for data-center services, gains from consolidation and improved efficiency are expected to plateau, with energy use resuming an upward trajectory subsequently.

Within the context of the current federal consolidation initiative, DOD's efforts are intended to address concerns about rising energy demands and costs of data centers, associated increases in carbon emissions, expanding real-estate footprints of data centers, and rising real-estate costs. According to DOD, it plans to reduce the number of its data centers by about 30% by 2013 (*Table 1*), and the number of servers by 25%. DOD intends to use savings generated from consolidation to pay the consolidation costs. It also plans to use cloud computing, where appropriate, as part of its consolidation and money-saving efforts.

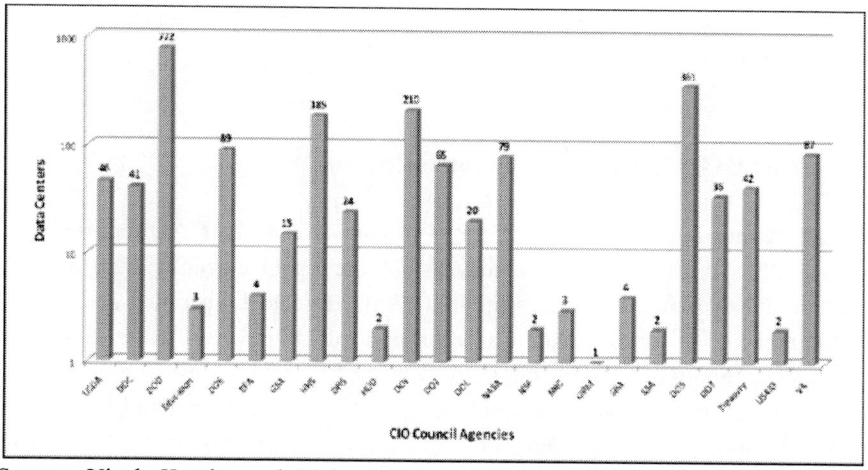

Source: Vivek Kundra and Richard Spires, "Update on the Federal Data Center Consolidation Initiative," Memorandum for Chief Information Officers, October 1, 2010.

Figure 3. Distribution of Federal Data Centers among Agencies, July 2010.

Table 1. Current DOD Data Centers and Reductions Planned by FY2013

	Current	Planned
Air Force	137	117
Army	250	154
Navy	78	77
Combatant Commands	25	21
Other	282	163
Total	772	532

Source: Department of Defense.

Note: Data for the "Other" category are tentative.

Further, also within DOD, the Defense Information Services Agency (DISA) has reportedly reduced its Defense Enterprise Computing Centers from 50 to 14 and is concentrating data centers on military bases as part of base realignment and closure. The Army began a major consolidation effort in 2006, although that project has faced obstacles, and the service has decided to use the DISA centers as part of its strategy. The Army capped data center growth in June 2010, concurrent with the government-wide announcement from the White House, and currently plans a 75% reduction, to 65 data centers by 2015. They did the same in January 2011, along with a planned 25%

reduction in data centers, and a planned increase in server use and virtualization.

Status of DOD Data Center Consolidation

In its July 2011 report on the status of the FDCCI, the GAO reported that both DOD's current asset inventory (what the DOD currently has) and its consolidation plan were incomplete. DOD released its own report in November 2011[23] that provided an overview of DOD activities, but did not address the recommendations made by GAO.

Although no specific assessment of DOD has been conducted, GAO has published its findings regarding duplicative IT investments by the DOD and DOE and discusses the FDCCI within the context of overall IT reform.[24]

RELATED ACTIVITY IN THE 113TH CONGRESS

On January 22, 2013, the House Committee on Oversight and Government Reform held a hearing on reforming IT spending in the federal government.[25] Witnesses in that hearing were Mr. Steven VanRoekel, Federal CIO, OMB; Mr. David Powner, Director, IT Management Issues, GAO; Mr. Douglas Bourgeois, Vice President, Chief Cloud Executive, VMware, Inc.; Mr. Michael Klayko, Advisor and Former CEO, Brocade Communications Systems, Inc.; and Mr. Chris Niehaus, Director, Office of Civic Innovation, Microsoft Corporation. The hearing was intended to examine perceived problems with IT procurement and what could be done to rectify them.

ISSUES FOR CONGRESS

Achieving effective Congressional oversight of the FDCCI will require awareness of the program and an understanding of the management challenges and policy considerations involved with data center consolidation. Additionally, Congress may wish to examine the current "reach" of the FDCCI and consider whether expanding the initiative to include other agencies, as the GAO has recommended, is appropriate.

FDCCI Awareness

Although this report discusses the DOD's implementation of the FDCCI, the initiative applies to 24 federal departments and agencies.

There is no single committee that has jurisdiction over the FDCCI; therefore, unlike many programs that are overseen by a single committee in each the Senate and the House, implementation of the FDCCI may require oversight by any number of committees with legislative jurisdiction. Although committees are experts on the departments and agencies they oversee, they may need additional expertise to understand and assess the impact of technologies such as data centers and cloud computing. Awareness throughout Congress of the consolidation initiative, as well as the general management challenges and policy considerations issues outlined below, may also assist committees in achieving effective oversight and, from GAO's assessments, oversight is necessary. GAO has repeatedly stated that

> moving forward to consolidate obviously redundant or underutilized centers is warranted— and should result in immediate cost savings and increased efficiency ... the success of the initiative will be based, in large part, on continued efforts to oversee the development of complete inventories and comprehensive consolidation plans. Without either, there is an increased risk that departments and agencies will be ill-prepared to manage a transformation as significant as that which has been proposed by the Federal CIO. Such a lack of preparation could slow the consolidations and reduce expected savings and efficiencies.[26]

Data Center Consolidation Management Challenges and Policy Considerations

Any organization consolidating its data centers, whether in the private or public sector, will have up-front costs. Investing in those costs can provide many benefits, but challenges do exist and need to be closely monitored by managers and policymakers alike.

Up-Front Costs versus Ongoing Savings

Departments and agencies participating in the FDCCI will have some up-front costs, such as moving or replacing hardware and upgrading facilities, and the disposition of facility leases and equipment (leased or owned). While there appears to be a consensus that the ongoing operational savings can substantially outweigh such initial costs, that may not always be the case, and there is some evidence that such efforts may be difficult, complicated by factors such as incompatible hardware and a procurement process that may create barriers to consolidation. Actual ongoing operational savings will depend on several factors. Policymakers may find it difficult to determine these savings in the absence of accurate and complete baseline measurements of energy and other costs. The FDCCI requires that plans include an explicit cost-benefit analysis. However, such an analysis requires either metering of data-center energy use or accurate estimates derived from modeling efforts. Neither source of information seems to be available for most federal data centers.

The focus of the effort is also important. For example, a consolidation project that focuses on hardware savings may result in much lower savings than one that also includes operations and other costs.

Maintaining Data Security

The reliance on cloud computing as an alternative to data centers could have a negative impact on data security if the consolidation process is not managed correctly. Consolidation will result in an increase in the number of users relying on any particular data center. Under some parts of the federal initiative, that will include other agencies. However, security was considered the biggest obstacle to such efforts by half of the respondents to a 2009 survey of federal agencies (more than four times higher than other factors such as cost). While improved security is cited as part of the rationale for the consolidation initiative, it is not clear how the security challenges it poses and the concerns expressed in the survey will be addressed. In the case of cloud computing, in contrast, the CIO Council responded to such concerns by establishing a specific security effort called the Federal Risk and Authorization Management Program (FedRAMP).[27] That program might also be relevant to the consolidation initiative.

Facilities Design and Energy Savings

The large overall percentage of data-center energy expended for cooling (see *Figure 1*) has focused increased attention on the role of facilities' design and operation. Specific criteria to increase the energy efficiency of data centers will be included in the new version of the LEED or similar industry rating system for green buildings. The Energy Star program has also developed an initiative to promote energy-efficient facilities design. A number of legislated mandates and executive branch policies continue to foster improved federal building energy efficiency and reduce federal energy use, with no exceptions made for data centers.

In its 2007 report, EPA had projected that national data-center energy use would double nearly twice between 2000 and 2011, and represent 100 billion kWh annually at a cost of $7.4 billion. A number of factors call EPA's estimates into question, including the lack of accurate metering by data centers and the aggregation of center electricity costs with their host facilities. Therefore, it was not possible to determine the likelihood that the estimate was either too high or too low. Even if the energy-use projection is accurate, the cost estimate might be low given increases in electricity rates.

Options for FDCCI Oversight by Congress

The appropriate Congressional committee may wish to monitor the progress of the department or agency under its jurisdiction. It may do this by holding hearings; requesting review of an agency's status through either the agency itself or a GAO study; or assessing the department or agency's progress and projected goals against the stated goals of the FDCCI.

Hearings

The OMB oversees the management of the FDCCI at the agency level. As such, it is the central point of information regarding the status of agency planning and implementation. More importantly, if OMB management practices are lacking in any way, the impact will be far reaching, potentially having a negative impact on the performance of all agencies as they implement their FDCCI plans. Consistent Congressional review of OMB's management practices could help detect and correct problems sooner than they might with that review. Committees may also wish to hold hearings to receive status reports directly from the CIO of the department or agency under their jurisdiction.

Review of Department and Agency FDCCI Plans and Assessments

As plans to consolidate data centers within the federal government are created and implemented, policymakers may want to monitor how departments and agencies are following the federal directives and responding to GAO assessments. Such monitoring can be achieved through assessments conducted internally by the department or agency itself or externally by GAO or the committee of jurisdiction.

Review of Internal Status Reports

Congress may monitor individual departments' and agencies' implementation of the FDCCI through regular reporting. For example, DOD released its own report in November 2011[28] that provided an overview of DOD activities, but did not address the recommendations made by GAO. Congress may want to provide more specific direction regarding the content of such reports, e.g., requiring a response to GAO findings in department and agency status reports.

Review of External Status Reports

Congress may also request that GAO conduct regular reviews of department and agency FDCCI progress. GAO reported comprehensively on the status of the overall progress of the FDCCI in its July 2011 report, but has not provided any department or agency-specific reports. Such reports might be able to be produced more quickly and released as they are completed, rather than in one report containing the status off all the departments and agencies. The committee of jurisdiction may also decide to conduct its own investigation.

Expansion of the FDCCI

The GAO has also recommended that the FDCCI could be expanded to include other members of the Chief Information Officer Council, such as the Office of the Director of National Intelligence, and other independent executive branch agencies, such as the Securities and Exchange Commission and the Federal Communications Commission. Congress may wish to explore the feasibility, benefits, and drawbacks of that suggestion and make its own recommendations.

APPENDIX A. RELATED LAWS

There are eight laws related to federal energy and data center management.

National Energy Conservation Policy Act[29]

P.L. 95-619

Consolidated Omnibus Budget Reconciliation Act of 1985[30]
P.L. 99-272

The 1978 National Energy Conservation Policy Act (NECPA , P.L. 95-619) initiated a program of retrofitting federal buildings to improve energy efficiency. It also required federal agencies, including DOD, to report annually on its progress in meeting energy consumption goals for facilities. The Consolidated Omnibus Budget Reconciliation Act of 1985 (also called the Deficit Reduction Act, P.L. 99-272) amended NECPA by authorizing energy savings contracts of up to 25 years. The 1992 Energy Policy Act (P.L. 102-486) further amended NECPA by adopting Energy Savings Performance Contracts (ESPCs) that offered federal agencies a novel means of making energy efficiency improvements to aging buildings and facilities (see discussion below).

Federal Energy Management Improvement Act of 1988[31]
P.L. 100-615

The Federal Energy Management Improvement Act of 1988 (P.L. 100-615) amended NECPA by requiring each agency to achieve a 10% reduction in energy consumption in federal buildings by FY1995 when measured against an FY1985 baseline in terms of British thermal units per gross square foot of building area. By FY2005, DOD reported a 28.3% reduction in energy consumption compared to the FY1985 baseline. Federal agencies report their energy consumption annually to Congress through FEMP.

Energy Policy Act of 1992[32]
P.L. 102-486

Authorized energy savings performance contracts of up to 25 years.

Energy Policy Act of 2005[33]
P.L. 109-58

Section 103 of EPACT (Energy Use Measurement and Accountability) amended Section 543 of NECPA by mandating advanced meters in federal buildings by October 1, 2012, to assist in reducing electricity use. Advanced meters have the capability to measure and record interval data (at least hourly for electricity), and to communicate the data to a remote location in a format that can be easily integrated into an advanced metering system. Section 103 requires at least daily data collection capability. Advanced metering offers the means to measure, verify, and optimize performance, including diagnosing equipment and systems operations, and to thereby promote energy use awareness for building managers and occupants. However, the EPACT requirement applies to entire buildings, not data centers within those buildings. Section 922 established a DOE research and development program to improve energy efficiency of data centers and other high energy-density facilities. Also, Section 104 established the requirement that federal agencies purchase Energy Star or FEMP-designate products discussed in the section on "Data-Center Power Consumption."

To Study and Promote the Use of Energy Efficient Computer Servers in the United States[34]
P.L. 109-431

Required the Administrator of the Environmental Protection Agency, through the Energy Star program, to study and report on the rapid growth and energy consumption of computer data centers by the federal government and private enterprise. The EPA responded with Report to Congress on Server and Data Center Energy Efficiency (August 2, 2007).

Energy Independence and Security Act of 2007[35]
P.L. 110-140

Section 431 (Energy Reduction Goals for Federal Buildings) amended the National Energy Conservation Policy Act (NECPA) by mandating a 30% energy reduction in federal buildings by 2015 relative to a 2005 baseline. Section 432 (Management of Energy and Water Efficiency in Federal Buildings) required DOE to issue guidelines and criteria that each federal agency will follow for designating "covered facilities," assigning energy managers, and implementing comprehensive energy and water evaluations. For the purpose of energy and water evaluations, covered facilities constitute at least 75% of facility energy use at each facility. Section 434 (Management of Federal Building Efficiency) required that federal agencies ensure the energy life-cycle cost effectiveness of major equipment replacements (such as heating and cooling systems) and renovations or expansion of existing space. Section 453 (Energy Efficiency for Data Center Buildings) established a joint DOE-EPA national information program on data-center energy efficiency.

Intelligence Authorization Act for FY2010[36]
P.L. 111-259

Sec. 414 (Plan to Implement Recommendations of the Data Center Energy Efficiency Reports) directed the National Intelligence Director to develop a plan to implement the recommendations of the study completed under P.L. 109-431.

APPENDIX B. RELATED EXECUTIVE ORDERS

There are three Executive Orders related to energy management.

Energy Efficient Standby Power Devices
Executive Order 13221, signed by President Bush on August 2, 2001

Requires federal agencies to purchase products that use no more than one watt in standby power consuming mode when purchasing commercially available, off-the-shelf products that use external standby power devices or that contain an internal standby power function.

If such products are not available, agencies must purchase products with the lowest standby power wattage while in their standby power consuming mode.

Requires agencies to adhere to this Order when life-cycle cost-effective and practicable, and where the relevant product's utility and performance are not compromised as a result.

Requires, beginning December 31, 2001, and on an annual basis thereafter, the Department of Energy, in consultation with the Department of Defense and the General Services Administration, to compile a preliminary list of products to be subject to these requirements.

Requires that the Department of Energy finalize the list and remove products deemed inappropriate for listing.

Strengthening Federal Environmental, Energy, and Transportation Management37 Executive Order 13423, signed by President Bush, January 24, 2007

Instructs federal agencies to conduct their environmental, transportation, and energy-related activities under the law in support of their respective missions in an environmentally, economically, and fiscally sound, integrated, continuously improving, efficient, and sustainable manner.

The Order sets goals in the area of electronics stewardship, among others.

Federal Leadership In Environmental, Energy and Economic Performance[38] Executive Order 13514, signed by President Obama Oct 5, 2009

Requires that federal agencies take further steps to ensure that their IT purchases are energy efficient or otherwise environmentally friendly.

Specifically requires federal agencies to promote electronics stewardship, in particular by implementing best management practices for energy-efficient management of servers and federal data centers.

End Notes

[1] The FDCCI homepage is at http://www.cio.gov/pages.cfm/page/FDCCI.

[2] For example, in 2006, federal servers and data centers consumed an estimated 6 billion kilowatt-hours (kWh) of electricity, an amount which was expected to double by 2011. In addition, in FY2010, about 30% of total federal IT investment was reportedly spent on data center infrastructure, even though agencies used less than 30% of available server capacity on average. Report to Congress on Server and Data Center Energy Efficiency, U.S. Environmental Protection Agency, ENERGY STAR Program, August 2, 2007, p. 7, http://www.energystar.gov/ia/partners/prod_development/downloads/EPA_Datacenter_ Re port_Congress_Final1.pdf, EPA Report.

[3] "EPEAT" is the Electronic Product Environmental Assessment Tool, an environmental rating system for electronic products designed to help evaluate, compare, and select environmentally preferable products. See http://www.epa.gov/ epp/pubs/products/epeat.htm.

[4] Data Center Operational Efficiency Best Practices, IBM Global Technology Services, p. 3, January 2012, http://public.dhe.ibm.com/common/ssi/ecm/en/rlw03007usen/RLW03007 USEN.PDF [Requires sign-up].

[5] EPA Report, p. 7.

[6] The National Institute of Standards and Technology defines VOIP as the delivery of voice services via packetized data services.

[7] Online at http://www.gpo.gov/fdsys/pkg/PLAW-109publ431/pdf/PLAW-109publ431.pdf.

[8] All information about this report is online at http://www.energystar.gov/index.cfm?c= prod_development.server_efficiency_study.

[9] Online at http://www.whitehouse.gov/assets/documents/2009fedleader_eo_rel.pdf.

[10] The FDCCI Homepage is at http://www.cio.gov/pages.cfm/page/FDCCI.

[11] Update on the Federal Data Center Consolidation Initiative, Executive Office of the President, October 2010, http://www.cio.gov/documents/State-of-the-Federal-Datacenter-Consolidation-Initiative-Report.pdf.

[12] "Green IT" refers to environmentally sound computing practices that can include a variety of efforts, such as using energy efficient data centers, purchasing computers that meet certain environmental standards, and recycling obsolete electronics.

[13] Appendix A contains a summary of laws that compose the federal framework for energy conservation. Appendix B contains a summary of Executive Orders that complement the federal framework for energy conservation.

[14] For example, in 2006, federal servers and data centers consumed an estimated 6 billion kilowatt-hours (kWh) of electricity, an amount which was expected to double by 2011. In addition, in FY2010, about 30% of total federal IT investment was reportedly spent on data center infrastructure, even though agencies used less than 30% of available server capacity on average.

[15] The 24 participating departments and agencies are Agriculture, Commerce, Defense, Education, Energy, Health and Human Services, Homeland Security, Housing and Urban Development, Interior, Justice, Labor, State, Transportation, Treasury, Veterans Affairs, Environmental Protection Agency, General Services Administration, National Aeronautics and Space Administration, National Science Foundation, Nuclear Regulatory Commission, Office of Personnel Management, Small Business Administration, Social Security Administration, and U.S. Agency for International Development.

[16] Online at http://www.whitehouse.gov/sites/default/files/omb/budget/fy2013/assets/spec.pdf.

[17] Online at http://www.cio.gov/documents/25-Point-Implementation-Plan-to-Reform-Federal%20IT.pdf.

[18] See http://www.cio.gov/pages.cfm/page/IT-Reform-Task-Force-Will-Drive-Data-Center-Closures. A detailed status report on the progress in closing data centers is available online at https://explore.data.gov/Federal-GovernmentFinances-and-Employment/Federal-Data-Center-Consolidation-Initiative-FDCCI/d5wm-4c37?.

[19] The National Institute for Standards and Technology defines "cloud computing" as "a model for enabling ubiquitous, convenient, on-demand network access to a shared pool of configurable computing resources (e.g., networks, servers, storage, applications, and services) that can be rapidly provisioned and released with minimal management effort or service provider interaction." Additional detail is available online at http://csrc.nist.gov/publications/nistpubs/800-145/ SP800-145.pdf.

[20] "Data Center Consolidation: Agencies Need to Complete Inventories and Plans to Achieve Expected Savings," GAO-11-565, GAO, July 2011, http://www.gao.gov/products/GAO-11-565. "Data Center Consolidation." Another report was published previously, "Opportunities to Reduce Potential Duplication in Government Programs, Save Tax Dollars, and Enhance Revenue," GAO-11-318SP, March 2011, http://www.gao.gov/products/GAO-11-318SP.

[21] "Information Technology Reform: Progress Made; More Needs to Be Done to Complete Actions and Measure Results," GAO-12-745T, GAO, May 24, 2012, http://www.gao.gov/products/GAO-12-745T.

[22] "Managing for Results: GAO's Work Related to the Interim Crosscutting Priority Goals under the GPRA Modernization Act," GAO-12-620R, GAO, May 31, 2012, http://www.gao.gov/products/GAO-12-620R. "GAO Report, Managing for Results."

[23] 2011 Data Center Consolidation Plan and Progress Report, November 2011, DOD, http://dodcio.defense.gov/Portals/0/Documents/FDCCI-Final-2011.pdf. "2011 DOD Report."

[24] Departments of Defense and Energy Need to Address Potentially Duplicative Investments, GAO, February 2012, http://www.gao.gov/assets/590/588656.pdf.

[25] "Wasting Information Technology Dollars: How Can the Federal Government Reform its IT Investment Strategy?," January 22, 2013, http://oversight.house.gov/hearing/wasting-information-technology-dollars-how-can-the-federalgovernment-reform-its-it-investment-strategy/.

[26] GAO Report, Managing for Results, pp. 54-55.

[27] The Federal Risk and Authorization Management Program (FedRAMP) is a government-wide program that provides a standardized approach to security assessment, authorization, and continuous monitoring for cloud products and services. This approach uses a "do once, use many times" framework that will save cost, time, and staff required to conduct redundant agency security assessments. FedRAMP was established on December 8, 2011, via an official memorandum from the Federal Chief Information Officer to all agency CIOs. For additional information, see http://www.gsa.gov/portal/category/102371.

[28] 2011 DOD Report.

[29] Online at http://www1.eere.energy.gov/femp/regulations/necpa.html and http://uscode.house.gov/download/pls/ 42C91.txt.

[30] A summary of this law is online at http://goo.gl/a6p9j.

[31] A summary of this law is online at http://goo.gl/kiZKF.

[32] Online at http://www1.eere.energy.gov/femp/regulations/epact1992.html.

[33] Online at http://www1.eere.energy.gov/femp/regulations/epact2005.html.

[34] Online at http://www.gpo.gov/fdsys/pkg/PLAW-109publ431/pdf/PLAW-109publ431.pdf.

[35] Online at http://www1.eere.energy.gov/femp/regulations/eisa.html.

[36] Online at http://www.gpo.gov/fdsys/pkg/PLAW-111publ259/pdf/PLAW-111publ259.pdf.

[37] Online at http://www.epa.gov/oaintrnt/practices/eo13423.htm.

[38] Online at http://www.epa.gov/oaintrnt/practices/eo13514.htm.

INDEX

A

B

C

D

E

F

G

H

I

J

L

M

N

O

P

R

W

Y